When Bad Things Happen, God Still Loves

When Bad Things Happen, GOD STILL LOVES

JOE BLAIR

BROADMAN PRESS
Nashville, Tennessee

4250-10
ISBN: 0-8054-5010-6
Dewey Decimal Classification: 231.6
Subject Headings: LOVE (THEOLOGY) // CHRISTIAN LIFE
Library of Congress Catalog Number: 85-13240
Printed in the United States of America

Unless otherwise stated, all Scripture references are from the Revised Standard
Version of the Bible, copyrighted 1946, 1952, © 1971, 1973.

Library of Congress Cataloging in Publication Data

Blair, Joe, 1941-
  When bad things happen, God still loves.

  1. Love—Religious aspects—Christianity. 2. God.
3. Theodicy. I. Title.
BV4637.B53 1986   231'.8   85-13240
ISBN 0-8054-5010-6

To
Carrie and Brad
Wife and Son
Who Express
God's Love

Contents

Foreword

People ask the hardest questions about God and life. Sometimes the question does not sound like a question, but a statement with a big question behind it. Strangely, most of the questions and statements that I encounter relate to this question, Who is God and how does He relate to me in this world where I see a mixture of the bad and good? Someone has said that life questions us. It does, and it forces us to ask the question about God and His relationship to us as well as our relationship to Him.

Too often God has been viewed as the antagonist of the human race. To some people, God is accuser, punisher, and even executioner. People who believe about God in that way cannot really abandon themselves in trust to Him with any degree of joy and security. How can they, when God is viewed as being against them, not for them?

This book may provide a framework for thinking about God in a way which I believe is the principal thrust of the Bible and the Christian faith: God is love and His way with us is the way of love. Life, however, with all its bad as well as its good, questions that conclusion. What follows is an effort to meet some of the tough questions head-on.

Ultimately no one can define, answer, or explain it all. God is more than we. He is above and beyond us as well as with us, and, as Martin Luther said, God sometimes does a "strange work." However, although we cannot explain it all, I am con-

9

vinced that there is every reason to stake one's life on the belief that God is love and His way with us is the way of love. God always "shows his love for us" (Rom. 5:8).

Acknowledgment is given and appreciation is expressed to several people for helping with this book: to Mrs. Betty Rogers, who typed the manuscript through several drafts; to friends such as Malcolm Tolbert and Fisher Humphreys who gave helpful insights and suggestions; to my wife Carrie for being a constant source of encouragment, as well as an insightful, stimulating critic of my work.

H. Joseph Blair
First Baptist Church
Ruston, Louisiana

1

Love, the Way of God with You

The love of God is infinitely more than what we call love in earthly relationships. It is much as more and different as God is more and different than man. He is the subject who determines the content of this love. The concept of love does not determine what God is, but God determines what love is. He is the subject and love the predicate. (Hendrikus Berkhof).[1]

I am afraid of what God will do to me (A church member).

God shows his love for us (Rom. 5:8).

The college student's face betrayed her. Even her smile could not hide the fact that she was troubled. Her words revealed an underlying anger and fear toward God. She was afraid to admit these feelings even to herself, perhaps because she feared that God might become angry, reject her, or do something worse. Did God really kill her brother as she thought, taking his life because of his rebelliousness? And how long would it be before enough wrong piled up in her life for God to strike her down? Or her parents, or her friend? Her conversation and questions reflected a conflict within, and she was having great difficulty reconciling her Christian faith with her brother's accidental death. Did God do this to her brother?

A Question

The college student sought an answer to a question which many people ask in one way or another: How does God relate to me? What is His way with me and others? The answers to this question are so important, because they determine how a person is going to think about God. Will I simply fear God, not in the sense of respect or reverence, but in the sense of sheer terror? If we believe in God and we believe that God is against us or ready to be against us at the slightest excuse, then we are in a losing situation. Who can stand against the power and authority of One who called the universe into existence? Will I look upon God as being against me rather than for me?

Will I believe God to be my light, my salvation, my stronghold (Ps. 27:1), or will I consider Him as the One who takes away my strength? Will I consider Him to be my hiding place and my shield (Ps. 119:114), or will I believe Him to be the One from whom I need protection and from whom I must flee? Will I believe Him to be my fortress, my rock (Ps. 18:2), or will I think of Him as the One before whom I tremble in insecurity? Will I consider God to be a very present help in trouble (Ps. 46:1), or will I believe Him to be my trouble? The kind of relationship I have with God from my side is determined by how I think about Him—what I believe Him to be like in relationship to me. Of course, the way God is to us is determined by Him from His side. What is God's way with me, with us?

Ultimately this question cannot be evaded. God as Creator and Sovereign Ruler over this world acts upon every life. The psalmist wondered where one could go to escape the presence of God. His conclusion: there is no escape. He said,

If I ascend to heaven, thou art there!
If I make my bed in Sheol, thou art there!
If I take the wings of the morning
    and dwell in the uttermost parts of the sea,
even there thy hand shall lead me,
and thy right hand shall hold me (Ps. 139:8-12).

The psalmist was happy that he could not escape the presence of God. Many people, however, because of misconceptions of God's way with us, wish they could escape. They fear that God is out to get His "pound of flesh" in order to balance the scales of righteousness.

Leslie Weatherhead was visiting in a home where a young son had died. He had died of cholera, one of the many victims in a spreading epidemic. John, the father, and Weatherhead paced up and down as they shared the grief together. Commenting at last as he searched for some explanation for the tragedy, the father said, "Well, Padre, it is the will of God. That's all.there is to it. It is the will of God."[2]

What was the man saying? Was he not saying that God had taken a cholera germ and placed it in the system of the small, defenseless boy so that he would die? Is this the way God acts upon life? Can God be trusted if He infects children with cholera germs? Could John really trust God if he believed that God, in a deliberate act, had taken the life of his son? To say that this death happened in the domain of God's world is one thing; to say that God did it is another thing entirely.

Weatherhead gently attempted to bring his friend to a different view. Pointing to John's daughter sleeping under a mosquito net on the porch, Weatherhead asked what he would do to someone who deliberately put a cholera-soaked cotton pad over his daughter's mouth. John reacted angrily, out of his love for his daughter, claiming that he would kill such a person with no more hesitation than he would a snake and throw him away. "But John, Weatherhead said, isn't that just what you have accused God of doing when you said it was his will? Call your little boy's death the result of mass ignorance, call it mass folly, call it mass sin, if you like, call it bad drains or communal carelessness, but don't call it the will of God."[3]

I have heard the stories firsthand. A child darts in front of a truck and is killed. Some said that God did it ("It was God's will"). An invalid died in a fire in his home, and some said that God did it. A teenager crashed his motorcycle in the middle of the night and no one found him until the next morning. He later died. Some said that God did it.

Is this the way God relates to us? Is it dangerous to be on God's side? Insurance companies describe certain disastrous acts of nature as "acts of God." That interpretation too often describes present-day attitudes. Is God a "bad risk?" Will He turn on you at any moment? Not even the insurance companies, according to their view of the way God relates to us, will insure some of God's activity! What a bad press God gets! And what a bad reputation He has as a result of the bad press. And how unfortunate! Are people attracted to God if they believe that God is going to hit them with a hurricane at the first opportunity? We need to reject negative, inadequate views of God's way with us.

An Answer

How does God relate to us? The apostle John measured the relationship and concluded that "God is love" (1 John 4:8). John 3:16 says, "God so loved the world. . . ." Paul wrote, "God shows his love to us in that while we were yet sinners Christ died for us" (Rom. 5:8).

To say that God is love describes the character and content of the Supreme Life who acts upon us. To say that God loves the world is to say that God acts upon all the world with love, those who believe in Him and those who do not. To say that God shows His love in and through the death of His Son is to say that God goes to ultimate lengths, even to experiencing death in His Son, in loving the whole world.

Immediately we are gripped by an awareness that God's love is no ordinary love. One cannot say, "I love the way he looks," or "I love the Dallas Cowboys," or "I love lemonade," and mean the same kind of love about which John and Paul wrote. People "love" everything. They "love" boats and cabins by the lake. They "love" peanut butter sandwiches and hot fudge sundaes.

They "love" motorcycles, cars, and a nice summer day at the beach. Obviously, the word *love* is in need of definition.

One kind of love may be designated by the Greek word *erōs.* *Erōs* describes a love that is frequently related to self-centeredness in some way. The word *erotic,* for example, a word usually associated with sexual acts, comes from the word *erōs.* Often *erōs* is used to describe the selfish motivation leading to illicit sexual relationships.

However, *erōs* has a broader meaning than this. It is a kind of love which sees something of value in the object in view and tries to appropriate that value for itself. It can be good or bad. It is good, for example, to love the beauty in a flower and appropriate that beauty into one's enjoyment. A boy or girl "falling in love" sees the attraction in the other, and that is good as long as the *erōs* is not perverted into lust. *Erōs* has the character at times of what people call "romantic" love, and it does have its place in relationships.

By itself, however, when it is not dominated and guided by a stronger, better love, *erōs* tends to degenerate into selfishness. Its character tends to be that which uses the value in a person or thing for its own selfish purposes. A marriage, for example, based only on *erōs* will fail unless it grows quickly into a bigger kind of love.

Another kind of love is that described as *philos.* It is usually love associated with friendship love. An excellent example is seen in the relationship between David and Jonathan in the Old Testament. Each loved the other as his own life (1 Sam. 18:1,3), a friendship which demonstrates the deepest level of *philos.*

Philos can be a love of varying levels. It can be used of people in a general sense with whom there is mutual respect and acceptance. Jesus so uses the word in Luke 14:12, as He told His host that He should not invite His "friends" (*philous*) to a banquet but those who are needy. The parable of Luke 11:5-8, where *philos* occurs four times, uses the word in the sense of "good neighbor" or "guest." Jesus addressed His disciples as "my friends" (*philois,* Luke 12:4), which reflected the teacher-student relationship as well as the deeper fellowship exhibited by Jesus' willingness to give Himself in their behalf.[4]

Also, fellow Christians sometimes were referred to as *philous.* In 3 John 15, for example, we read: "Peace be to you. The friends [*philoi*] greet you. Greet the friends [philous], every one of them." This was certainly an expression of endearment.[5]

The Christian faith is a community faith as well as an individual faith. The faith we encounter in the community of friends helps to sustain and strengthen our faith. And how we need such faithful friends! I am indebted to the community of faith in which I was raised. The local church of which I was part affirmed me in every way. They worshiped with me. They taught me about God and His revelation of Himself in Jesus Christ. They lived the faith before me. Certain adults, along with my parents, took an interest in me as a teenager and supported some of the decisions about my life's direction. My experience since that time has been one in which I have continued to encounter people in the community of faith who related to me with *philos* love.

Friendship love reflects a mutual respect and acceptance expressed at different levels. It is a good kind of love to know and express. It also is good to know that this kind of love is legitimate when exercised at various levels. We can't be as close to all people as we can to some, but we can show friendship love to all. In that sense we can have an attitude of friendship love toward the world, even the world from which distance separates us. It is much better to approach the world with an attitude of friendship than with an attitude of suspicion and hostility. However, what happens to this *philos* love when we encounter enemies in the world?

Philos, like *erōs,* can be exercised wrongly. Friendship love, as good as it may be, is not enough. It can be rather exclusive;

it can draw lines. We tend to count as friends only those of our group, our color, or our culture. It can be encouraging to those who are included but discouraging and even destructive to those who are excluded. *Philos* is not strong enough to break through the barriers of race, class, color, nationality, and other barriers which separate people from people.

What is the content and character of God's relationship to us? Is God's love *erōs?* Does God simply look upon us as valuable objects to use for His ends? We are valuable in His eyes, of course, and *erōs* used in this limited way is correct. But is that value simply there so long as we please Him? When we sin, rebel against Him, are we then thrown away as so much damaged merchandise? Some people are afraid that this is true, but the biblical witness gives a decided no. God's love is not selfish *erōs*. *Erōs* is simply too narrow to describe God's kind of relationship. Human beings are not puppets which God manipulates for His selfish gratification. And God's involvement with us is not simply limited to an objective evaluation that we are valuable.

Is *philos* the content and character of the Father who relates to us? God certainly is friendly toward us, and He counts us as His friends. Does God love only a certain group, a certain culture, or a certain color? Does God have favorites? Some are afraid that He does. People place themselves outside God's love because they have failed (sinned) in some way, and the result is that they believe God is not friendly toward them. They think they are not among God's favorites. The Bible gives witness that God "shows no partiality" (Rom. 2:11), nor does He exclude anyone on the basis of race, color, sex, or status (Gal. 3:28). *Philos* is too narrow to describe the character and content of God's love. Even in its best sense, when you will give yourself for your friends, *philos* does not describe the depths of God's love, because He gave Himself for His enemies.

A Special Love

Agapē is the word we need. *Agapē* is a word used in the New Testament to describe God's love. "God shows his [*agapē*] to us" (Rom. 5:8). Into this word is poured the highest concept to love which human minds can conceive.

Agapē is unselfish. It is outgoing. It is life directed outward away from self for the enhancement of other life. Giving and sharing what one is with another is the essence of *agapē*. "God is [*agapē*]" (1 John 4:8).

> He can acquire nothing because he is God. He needs nothing because he is God. He has all goodness and all riches within himself. But goodness is self-diffusive; it seeks to share itself. So the infinite goodness which is God seeks to communicate, to diffuse, to share itself . . . with you . . . with me . . . with all of us.[6]

Agapē is unmotivated by outward pressures or considerations. It has its nature and origin in God. One cannot cause *agapē* to be evoked in the nature of God. *Agapē* is the nature of God—His essence. C. H. Dodd emphasized that love isn't simply *one* of God's activities. Rather, all of His activity is loving activity. "If He creates, He creates in love; if He rules, He rules in love; if He judges, He judges in love. All that He does is the expression of His nature, which is—to love."[7] One does not cause God to love by the worthiness of acts, conditions, or attitudes. Love is there, as outgoing life from God acting upon our lives, completely on the initiative of God.

Agapē, of the nature that we have discussed thus far, has its origin in God. If we have *agapē* at all, it is because we have experienced it from God. Emil Brunner asked the origin of *agapē* love since it is an unmotivated love. He said that it cannot arise in us.

> What is in us must be motivated. In ourselves there is only the

possibility of eros, not of agape. Agape comes to us as God's gift and, more, as God's gift of himself.[8]

The fact that He gives Himself toward us cannot be thwarted. You can choose not to recognize the loving Being acting upon your being, but that does not stop God from doing so. It is up to each individual to accept or reject God's loving activity from personal experience. If you reject God, then you have judged yourself. The judgment is that you have separated yourself from the redeeming love of God. What have you done then but to identify yourself with that which is over against the redeeming love of God?

But, amazingly, even rejection does not stop God from loving someone. *Agapē* is also unconditional. God's *agapē* is extended to all humankind without exception. He does not only act upon a person when certain conditions are met; God loves completely, regardless of conditions. He may not approve the conditions, but He never stops reaching out to a person with love.

Simon Peter approached Jesus one day and asked, "Lord, how often shall my brother sin against me, and I forgive him? As many as seven times?" (Matt. 18:21). The topic was one discussed in religious circles of that time. Peter probably actually thought he was being rather liberal, for it seems that the general conclusion was that three times was enough. A person should not be forgiven the fourth time. Jesus replied that Peter should be willing to forgive "seventy times seven" (Matt. 18:22), which means an unlimited number of times.

The instruction about forgiveness arises out of the character and nature of God. "Seventy times seven" Represents what God has done toward us. Following this statement about forgiveness, Jesus told a parable (Matt. 18:23-35) to illustrate His point to Peter and the others. A servant owed his king ten thousand talents—an immense debt. The servant begged his king to have patience with him until he could pay, and out of pity for the servant, the king forgave the debt.

Later, that same servant found a fellow servant who owed him a hundred denarii—a much smaller amount. He demanded payment, and when payment could not be made, the fellow servant's pleas for patience fell on deaf ears, and the first servant had him thrown into jail. When the king found how the first servant had acted, he demanded that the unforgiving servant be put in jail.

The servant who had been forgiven so much was willing to forgive so little. The first servant's amount of debt, exaggerated by Jesus to make a point, was equivalent to about ten million dollars. The second servant owed the first servant an amount equal to about twenty dollars. God forgives us so much. Whatever we are called on to forgive about our brother, it is nothing compared to what we have been forgiven.

The point is that we should be willing to forgive. But shining through the statement about forgiveness and the parable Jesus told is the unlimited forgiveness of God. God never stops forgiving and loving us. The outstanding demonstration of that unlimited forgiveness growing out of an unlimited love is Jesus on the cross saying, "Father, forgive them; for they know not what they do" (Luke 23:34).

Psychiatrist Scott Peck, in his book *The Way Less Traveled*, captured the meaning of *agapē* in a modern definition of love: "The will to extend one's self for the purpose of nurturing one's own or another's spiritual growth."[9] It is work; it is expended energy; it is expended life. "It is a self-donation," John Powell said, "which may prove to be an altar of sacrifice."[10]

Exactly! God's *agapē* knows no limits. "God shows his love for us in that while we were yet sinners Christ died for us" (Rom. 5:8). Sinners? That means that God in Christ donated self (outgoing being) in behalf of those who were against Him, even His worst enemies. You might give yourself for your friends (Rom. 5:7), but for your enemies? *Agapē* does. Jesus said, "I came not to call the righteous, but sinners" (Mark 2:17). In commenting on this statement, Anders Nygren wrote, "With these words He

turns the entire scale of Jewish values upside down."[11] Some
thought, taught, and believed that God would come only to the
righteous. But Jesus came in a deliberate search for the unrighteous. What an unheard-of action!

"Love your enemies," Jesus said (Matt. 5:44), and He was not
simply talking about having goodwill toward them. It is easy
enough to love our enemies at a distance. What if God had loved
His enemies, loved us sinners, at a distance? He never would
have gotten involved with us in Jesus. God has never related to
His people, to the world, with only goodwill. He always has
involved Himself. Jesus expended Himself for His enemies in
both His living and His dying. When He instructs us to love our
enemies, He means for us to actively engage in expending ourselves for the good of those enemies.

Agapē, then, is unmotivated, unconditional, and unlimited.
Now we have answered our original question about the content
and character of God's way with us. It is not only *erōs* or *philos*,
and never in their perverted forms. It is *agapē*. *Erōs* and *philos*
are caught up and included in *agapē* so that they are never
selfish or narrow. God is *agapē*, and He is never exclusive or
narrow in His relationship with us.

But what are we doing with evil and suffering in this world
if God's way with us, the All-Powerful Creator, is love? What of
alienation from God, absence of community, death, judgment,
and other bad experiences of life? These questions are most
difficult, and we will attempt to answer them, but we must not
allow their difficulty to tear us away from our moorings. For
here is the foundation upon which we build a trusting relationship with the Father: God's way with us is the way of love.

Notes

1. Hendrikus Berkhof, *Christian Faith: An Introduction to the Study of the Faith*, trans, by Sierd Woudstra (Grand Rapids: William B. Eerdmans Publishing Company, 1979), p. 121.

2. Leslie D. Weatherhead, *The Will of God* (New York: Abingdon Press, 1934), p. 10.

3. Ibid, p. 11.

4. Gustav Stählin, *"philos,"* *Theological Dictionary of the New Testament,* IX, ed. by Gerhard Freidrich, trans. and ed. by Geoffrey W. Bromiley (Grand Rapids: Wm. B. Eerdmans Publishing Company, 1974), pp. 160-161.

5. Ibid, p. 166.

6. John Powell, *Why Am I Afraid to Love?* (Niles, Ill.: Argus Communications Co., 1972), p. 11.

7. C. H. Dodd, *The Johannine Epistles* (London: Hodder and Stoughton, 1946), p. 107.

8. Emil Brunner, *Faith, Hope, and Love* (Philadelphia: Westminster Press, 1956), p. 75.

9. Scott Peck, *The Way Less Traveled* (New York: Simon and Schuster, 1978), p. 81.

10. Powell, p. 108.

11. Anders Nygren, *Agape and Eros,* trans, by Philip S. Watson (London: S.P.C.K., 1953), p. 68.

2

Love and God's Toughness

God's loving is a divine being and action distinct from any other loving in the fact that it is holy. As holy, it is characterized by the fact that God, as He seeks and creates fellowship, is always the Lord. He therefore distinguishes and maintains His own will against every other will. (Karl Barth).[1]

When you talk about love, are you talking about some sentimental attitude in which a person is afraid of his own shadow? (A discussion leader).

God shows his love for us (Rom. 5:8).

When Cephas came . . . I opposed him to his face (Gal. 2:11).

Walter Shurden told of his private symbol of Christianity that goes all the way back to his elementary school days. A new boy had come to school, and the resident bully challenged the newcomer to a battle. The scraggly boy accepted the challenge. Word spread about the upcoming fight, and everyone met at the water fountain, the fighting arena for the grammar school. The spectators formed a circle, and the two squared off. It was obvious immediately that the newcomer's possibility of success was in doubt, because he made a fist with his thumb pressed over the top of the index finger. Real fighters don't make a fist that way. The bully hit the boy, knocking him down. The newcomer looked up from the ground, let out a mad cry, and wiped the blood, dirt, and spit from his mouth with the back of his hand. What happened at that point later became a symbol of faith for Shurden. The boy got to his feet and waded back into the bully.

Christians get bruised and hurt—knocked down—and do not want to get up and enter the fray again. But the Christian is called to struggle. As Shurden wrote, "You have to struggle to 'make' meaning. That is the testimony of all the saints of all the years."[2]

Life is tough, and the Christian life is especially tough. A person needs to be tough in order to live the Christian life. But how does love fit with that requirement of character? Is God tough? How does God who is love and calls us also to love fit into a tough, struggling world? Some people think that He does not, and they have left God out of their lives altogether. They still carry a concept of a meek and mild God who has nothing to say to a tough world.

Some people mistake love as an extreme passiveness in the face of life's demands. The person who loves is looked upon as something of a pushover. If we emphasize the essential nature of God's character as being love, is He a pushover?

I must admit that I used to struggle with the concept of love in relationship to the tough kind of living which life required. Some statements in a seminary lecture by Malcolm Tolbert started me in a new direction with my understanding of love: "To be a loving person does not mean that you are required to allow someone to make a doormat of you," he said.

I realized at that point that subconsciously I had been thinking that love was to be understood in those terms although consciously I had resisted the idea. Since my subconscious idea was in contrast to my conscious idea, a conflict had existed in my thinking which I had not bothered to identify and alleviate. To hear the words of Tolbert, then, was something of a liberating experience.

To allow someone to use us or manipulate us is a sin at its worst and cowardice at its best. To know that God the Creator loves us, gives us surpassing worth and dignity. If we understand that and accept it, then we expect to be treated as people of value and dignity.

Such love means, also, that others are to be treated with value and dignity. Tolbert presented a hypothetical case in which one is wronged by another. What approach could be taken? "You can help someone understand," Tolbert said, "that you think too much of him and of yourself to allow him to treat you that way."

Love Cares Enough to Confront

A confrontation made in the way Tolbert suggested, on the basis of God's love for us and God's love for the other person, can redeem and restore relationships. Such love, however, is a tough, confronting love, and many of us would rather that love did not demand that we confront. This is not to say that love doesn't sometimes keep quiet. Of course it does, and this, too, is very difficult to do. But we have less trouble understanding the quiet aspect of love than we do the tough, aggressive aspect of love. Most people have their greatest difficulty living by love at this very point. Only God's kind of love can help us.

We need to be honest with ourselves. Do we hold to a weak sentimentality we call love, which is not *agapē* love at all, so that we can have an excuse not to confront with tough love? Or, are we seeking to escape some struggle against some situation which tough love calls us to make? If we do so, we do not practice God's kind of love in our relationships, because God's love is not sentimentality and God's kind of love does not permit one to escape from living responsibly.

On the other hand, some of us can confront if we do not have to care about the other person when we do so. For then we can treat the other person as less than we are, and our confronting doesn't cost us anything. Sometimes, for example, a statement like this is made: "Let me be frank with you," and then begins a confrontation. Many times "let me be frank with you" means

"I am going to tell you my opinion and that is the important thing—that I tell my opinion. What happens to you after that simply does not concern me." Some have considered such frankness to be a virtue, but it is a self-centered kind of confrontation in reality.

Tough love is not like that. It cares about the other person. It respects the other person as one of worth and dignity. David Augsburger wrote beautifully about mutual respect necessary to right relationships and redeeming confrontations:

> When my thrust as a person—my hopes, dreams, wants, needs, drives—runs counter to your thrust, there is conflict. To sacrifice my thrust is to be untrue to the push and pull of God within me. To negate your thrust is to refuse to be reverent before the presence and work of God within you.[3]

Augsburger adds that caring enough to integrate the needs and wants of each other "toward creating Christian community is what effective living is about"[4] Augsburger means Christian community between two people as well as a larger group. This is exercising tough love.

But are we claiming too much for the kind of love we have discussed in this book? Have we exceeded the limits of *agape* when we speak of love's toughness? We have discussed the nature of God's sacrificial love as expended life in behalf of another. Is there room in that concept of love for a tough, confronting exercise of God's love? Obviously, I believe there is, and if we are to understand God's love, we must see the nature and need of its toughness.

Did Paul Love with Tough Love?

As I read Galatians 2:11-14, a rather amusing picture forms in my mind. I see the small, wiry, fiery Paul standing toe to toe with the burly apostle Peter, telling him that he has just goofed.

Before the men "from James" came, Peter sat at the table with Gentiles and shared their food. The men from James were a delegation from Jerusalem. They were followers of Christ, but they had not freed themselves completely from some Jewish customs which reflected prejudice against Gentiles. Apparently, James' disciples argued that to eat with Gentiles was to risk spiritual contamination.

The eating code elaborated in Leviticus 11 and Deuteronomy 14 describes at length what is clean and unclean food. The Jews, of course, were not to eat anything unclean. So, one of the problems with eating with the Gentiles, as far as Peter and his friends were concerned, was the fear they would eat something unclean and thus break the law. The Gentiles often were not familiar with the classes of unclean food.

In addition to the fear of food contamination, Peter and his friends feared that the fellowship around the table would be contaminated. The Jewish view was that the table became God's table since the meal was a time for giving thanks, sharing aspirations, discussing the Torah (the Law), and sharing the thoughts of God. What happened around the table made people family. James' men were convinced that the Gentiles were not spiritual enough to sit at the table with them.

Peter agreed with the visitors from Jerusalem and withdrew from table fellowship with the Gentiles. Peter did not act out of the love He had experienced in Christ Jesus; He acted out of a tradition of dietary rules and religious regulations. His actions created hostility and disunity in the church. Even dependable Barnabas followed Peter's example.

What does love do in a situation like that? It confronts. It gets tough. Paul, the great Apostle to the Gentiles, stood face to face with Peter, the great Apostle to the Jews, and told him he was wrong. Paul's actions and words called for inclusion of everyone on an equal basis into the church of the Lord Jesus Christ.

The basis for Paul's tough action in this situation is found in Galatians 2:20: "The life I now live in the flesh I live by faith in the Son of God, who loved me and gave himself for me." Peter fell back into an old way of thinking—that the keeping of the rules was the means by which a person could make his way to God. Paul had discovered that there was not a way of a person to God, but a way of God to a person. That way of God was Christ, who Paul said, "loved me and gave himself for me." Since this love of God came unearned and undeserved, Paul realized that it was for all people. God's love in Christ is for all regardless of their race, social status, or sex. Peter, then, worked against Christ by separating himself from his Gentile Christian friends, and in so doing denied God's love by which Peter himself had been accepted.

It was out of the love that he had experienced that Paul confronted Peter. Peter's actions were unacceptable. They were hurtful. Peter reduced the Gentiles to doormat status. He created division in the church. The love with which God loved would not allow the Gentiles to be treated that way nor would it allow Peter to act that way. Love made Paul confront Peter. His love was a tough, demanding love. He cared for the church of the Lord Jesus Christ enough to attempt to keep it away from racial bigotry. Paul cared for himself and his own mission enough to stand and state his case.

This was a crucial moment in the Christian movement. For Paul not to have loved with a tough love in this situation would have been selfish and a possible disaster for the Gentile Christians. The love which Paul had experienced and the love which he had for Christ demanded that he confront the situation with tough love.

Another example of Paul's tough love is seen in relationship to the Corinthian church. The Corinthians were most difficult to deal with. A number of internal problems within the church kept the church in turmoil.

Consider 2 Corinthians 2:1-4. Paul had visited with the Corinthians which had been a "painful" visit (v. 1). It had been a time of confrontation with those whom he loved. He next had sent a letter, to which he referred in verse 3. He wrote out of anguish and affliction of heart and with many tears, not to cause them pain, but because he wanted them to know of his "abundant love" for them (v. 4). Filson, in his commentary on 2 Corinthians, wrote, "Love must sometimes be stern, and this was such a time; but the love was in control."[5]

Or consider 2 Corinthians 11 and 12. Paul's apostleship and abilities were brought into question, and some tried to lead the Corinthians away from his leadership. He got tough with the Corinthians. Behind and in all the toughness, however, was love. In 11:11, he explained to the Corinthians that God knew how much Paul loved them. In 12:15, he affirmed that he would gladly spend and be spent for them. This may be interpreted in the sense that Paul was "ready to do more than a parent's duty, and to do it with delight. He will spend all he has and exhaust all his strength, for his children."[6]

Now remember, this is the Paul who had been a persecutor. Before meeting the Christ who loved and gave Himself for him, Paul dealt with his opponents with violence. He did not, however, deal with the troublesome Corinthians with violence or even rejection. He loved them with tough love, a love both demanding and accepting.

Did Jesus Love with Tough Love?

Jesus' toughness often has been overlooked. He has been presented rather negatively at times as a weak individual who allowed other people to use Him, to walk over Him as if He were only a doormat. Didn't they use Him as they wished at His trial and crucifixion?

At first glance that may seem true. However Jesus deliberately went to Jerusalem. He chose to go to Gethsemane where He knew He could be found and arrested; He chose to submit Himself to the trial and the brutal treatment of the soldiers; He deliberately chose the way of the cross. The situation was one in which this Son of love who was love Himself, aggressively confronted the worst that humankind could be and do.

As He stood before them at the trial and at the scourging, and as He hung before them on the cross, Jesus never accepted what they were doing and being. Amazingly, He confronted their guilt with His innocence, their violence with His nonviolence, their evil with His righteousness, and their unacceptance with His loving acceptance. Did He not say from the cross, "Father, forgive them; for they know not what they do" (Luke 23:34)? They were wrong and were doing wrong. Jesus did not accept that. He did confront their wrongness with love and forgiveness. He expressed to His Father—something which all the world needs to hear and follow—how He felt toward His enemies. He petitioned for their forgiveness. Submission to the trial, the scourging, and the cross were aggressive acts of tough, redemptive love on the part of Jesus.

Can anyone read about the cleansing of the Temple and doubt that Jesus loved with a tough love? He turned over the tables of the money changers and drove away the animals, clearing the outer worship area so the Gentiles could worship. I can imagine Him standing there in the center of that scene, fire in His eyes, saying: "It is written, 'My house shall be called a house of prayer'; but you make it a den of robbers" (Matt. 21:13). I am reminded, when I think of this incident, of what one preacher said about Jesus' cleansing of the Temple: "It was a very manly act."

Jesus did not hesitate to tell the truth with hard-hitting, forceful preaching. Read Matthew 23 to see His courageous, tough confrontation message to the scribes and Pharisees. Jesus had great compassion for sinners and outcasts. His message to them was one of acceptance and forgiveness. They seemed to know their need and were willing to admit their sinfulness. Rather than denouncing them, Jesus received them just as they were. It takes a tough love to receive people just as they are and begin from that point.

While Jesus was compassionate and patient with sinners, the religionists of His day—many of those among the scribes and Pharisees—needed a different approach. They had great need, were away from God, and did not know it. They were missing out on the love, forgiveness, and acceptance of God. Tough words spoken out of a tough love were needed. Jesus did so: "Woe to you Scribes and Pharisees."

Speaking like that and loving with tough love which really cares for others is costly. Rejection is risked, and Jesus was well aware of rejection because He experienced it. Also, there was the agonized concern of seeing those loved going in the wrong way. The last of the chapter (Matt. 23:37-39) is revealing. Jesus wanted to gather Jerusalem and the people of Israel to Himself. Jesus loved with a tough love even when it hurt.

Does God Love with Tough Love?

Some people believe God does not love with a tough love. They consider Him to be a benevolent Father who extends limitless indulgence to the children on planet Earth. He sort of looks the other way when humanity engages in folly and says, "Oh well, children will be children." Fisher Humphreys describes such misguided sentimentality in this way:

> God is a grandfatherly old fellow in the sky, smiling benignly on everything good or bad, and gushing syrupy, sugary nonsense to weak people who have a neurotic need to hear that sort of thing.[7]

Of course that description of God is a misconception of a loving God because it is a terrible misconception of love. Who among us would say of those whom we love, "I don't care what they do or what they become"? What father would say of his daughter, if he loves her, "I don't care if she becomes a thief, or an unethical politician, or an unfaithful wife or irresponsible mother"? No, a parent who truly loves invests his best energies, including discipline, into his child. Rollo May said, "Hate is not the opposite of love; apathy is."[8] Love is expended life in behalf of another. Parents who love unselfishly will involve themselves in constructive, healthy ways so that their children can reach their potential and become well-adjusted, fulfilled individuals.

How much more true is it that God loves His children with a love much greater than that of a parent. The writer of Hebrews said it in these terms: "For the Lord disciplines him whom he loves, and chastises every son whom he receives" (Heb. 12:6). This is not a mean discipline but a loving discipline. We call too many things God's discipline which are not (see the chapters on judgment). But there is no room for a sentimentality which we sometimes call love. Humphreys said:

> This view falls apart before God's love, a tough love, so tough that God would die for us. God's love isn't so permissive that anything is acceptable. Instead, God so determined to do right that he will not smile on evil, he will not ignore it or become implicated in it in any way, and he will consistently oppose it. We need to get rid of that sentimental stuff once and for all. Then maybe we'll begin to know God better.[9]

God confronts us when we engage in sinfulness. He has pointed out that sin hurts and destroys; it takes but does not give. Our miseries and misused lives tell us that. He does not let us escape our choices and actions. God is tough on us in this way. He will not let us delude ourselves for long; and even if we choose a wrong course of life, he will still confront us, sometimes in very tough ways in order to lead us in the "paths of righteousness" (Ps. 23:3).

We see an example of God's confrontation after Adam had sinned and had hidden himself from God. God asked Adam, as He came into the garden, "Where are you?" (See Gen. 3:1-9.) Now God knew where Adam was. His question was a confrontation question. The sense of the question might be expressed this way: "Now look what you have done to yourself, Adam. See what a dire circumstance you have gotten yourself into. It is a tragic thing you have done, Adam."

God would not let Adam hide from the reality of his choices and actions. Neither will He let us do so. In the words of the prophet He warns us, "There is a way which seems right to a man, but its end is the way of death" (Prov. 14:12). He confronts us and tries to keep us from those ways. He is very tough on us at this point; He will not allow us to be unrealistic.

God not only confronts, He expects or demands. Love is demanding of the beloved, not for the sake only of the one loving but for the sake of the beloved. In response to an article on alcoholism, a magazine received an anonymous letter. The letter explained that its author had grown up in a home with an alcoholic father. The author indicated that no one talked about the problem, and it was ignored as much as possible. Then the author wrote these revealing words: "Finally, I discovered 'Tough Love.' I confronted my dad with the facts . . . my dad entered a program to dry out . . . thanks to God and tough love my dad is dry now and has been for four years."[10]

The writer of the letter had placed love's tough demand on his dad. He was expected to be, for his own good first of all, the person who was not subject to his alcoholism. Love demanded that he be the person he was capable of being. For the same reason, God makes demands on us.

The commandments of God expressed in the actions and words of Jesus are the demands He places upon us. God wants us to follow His Son—to grow into the "measure of the stature of the fullness of Christ" (Eph. 4:13). To be like Christ is our aim. We are to love as Christ did and does. His love was a tough, self-giving love. No sacrifice was too great for Him to make, even for His enemies—so He died on the cross for all. At the same time, His respect and love for Himself, as well as His love for others, meant that He did not allow anyone to intimidate Him or manipulate Him. Also, when something had to be done or said for the good of someone else or Himself, He did or said whatever it was. However, His interest in Himself was never selfish.

We need to caution ourselves as we attempt to love with tough love as Christ did. We do need to discern when to keep quiet and when to speak, for there are those times. We do need to discern when to act and when to be still. We need to examine our motives to make certain we do not act from selfishness.

God, as we know Him in Jesus Christ, is primary as we are called to be mature followers of Christ and love with tough love. Norman Geisler indicated that love for God on our part may at times seem to be at variance with love for people. Sometimes it is necessary to be disobedient to the wishes of people in order to be obedient to the wishes of God. This does not mean that a person chooses God in place of choosing people. In fact, being disobedient to the wishes of people, even being against them at times, may be the best way to love them in some cases. We do not will the good of others by agreeing to give in to that which is wrong. To put God first is to put others first, or as Geisler said it, " . . . to love God more than others is to love the others more."[11]

One of the toughest demands of God upon us is that we love our enemies. God did, and does. His love is so tough that it withstands abuse, rejection, and even torture and death, as witness the experience of Jesus on the cross. He does not let even evil and hatred put limits on His love. Wallace Hamilton told of the experience of Bishop Arthur Moore who grew up in rural Georgia. When Moore as a boy sang with his church about a wideness in God's mercy being like the wideness of the sea, he pictured in his mind the millpond nearby. Later, when he traveled and sailed for days on end over the ocean, he thought of the wideness of God's mercy in terms of the vast, seemingly limitless ocean.[12]

God's love is so vast that it even includes His enemies. Is our love that tough, or do we let the evil limit the limits of our love? Who can fail to respect, that is worship, our God whose love is so tough that it withstands the worst that evil can dish out and remain unchanged. Yet His love changes the evil and slowly but surely determines the ultimate destiny of humankind. God loves with a tough love.

Notes

1. Karl Barth, *Church Dogmatics II, The Doctrine of God, I,* trans. by T.H.L. Parker, et. al., ed. by G. W. Bromiley and T. F. Torrence (New York: Charles Scribner's Sons, 1957), p. 359.

2. Walter B. Shurden, "On Making It to Dinner," *The Struggle for Meaning,* ed. by William Tuck (Valley Forge, Penn.: Judson Press, 1977), 104.

3. David Augsburger, *Caring Enough to Confront* (Glendale, Calif.: Regal Books, 1980), p. 6.

4. *Ibid.*

5. Floyd Filson, "The Second Epistle to the Corinthians: Introduction and Exegesis," *The Interpreter's Bible, Vol. X.* ed. by George Buttrick (New York: Abingdon Press, 1953), 294.

6. Alfred Plummer, *A Critical and Exegetical Commentary on the Second Epistle of St. Paul to the Corinthians, The International Critical Commentary,* ed. by S. R. Driver, G. Plummer, and C. A. Briggs, 2nd ed. (Edinburgh: T & T Clark, 1914), p. 362.

7. Fisher Humphreys, *The Almighty* (Elgin, Ill.: David C. Cook Publishing Co., 1976), p. 41.

8. Rollo May, *Love and Will* (New York: W. W. Norton & Company, Inc., 1969), p. 29.

9. Humphreys.

10. Letter to the editor, *Home Missions,* November, 1978, p. 64.

11. Norman Geisler, *The Christian Ethic of Love* (Grand Rapids: Zondervan, 1973), p. 32.

12. J. Wallace Hamilton, *Who Goes There?* (Westwood, N.J.: Fleming H. Revell Company, 1958), p. 128.

3

Love and the Sinner

Just when Paul is utterly alienated from God, and that not merely in the sense of *feeling* himself far from God, but in the sense that he *is* as far removed from God as possible—*just in his greatest sin God's calling and election came to him. That is Agape: that is God's way with man.* (Anders Nygren).[1]

Can God ever forgive me? (A seeker).

God shows his love for us in that while we were yet sinners Christ died for us (Rom. 5:8).

It is difficult sometimes to determine what motivates us to act as we do. For example, what motivated Paul to strike out so fiercely at the followers of Christ? Perhaps he decided to impress his superiors so he could move up the political and ecclesiastical ladder. Did he visualize himself in the future as a leading rabbi who would have religious and political power to make him among the very important in the nation? If so, putting down a heretical Jesus movement would have gained him great merit. Perhaps he really believed that Christ's followers were a threat to the purity of Judaism as he perceived it, and he set out to protect his faith. Or perhaps he had begun to doubt his own beliefs because of the truth and commitment he discovered in Christ's followers, and thus he was fighting his doubts by fighting Christ. Perhaps there was a reason even deeper than any of these.

The Need for Love

Simons and Reidy, in *The Risk of Loving,* claimed that "if there is a natural law for humans, it shows itself most clearly in our response to love. We all desperately long to be loved."[2] Each person desires to be seen as a person of value in the eyes of someone, or a number of someones. We may not realize sometimes that we are working so hard to be loved, for we say that we are committed to being successful, or to gaining significant recognition for our cause, or even to serving others. We labor under the idea that we will be loved if we are beautiful, rich, popular, or secure enough.

> For many of us, our need for love takes the form of a drive for achievement. Unaware of the source of our efforts, we may write books, give lectures, earn titles, and transform economics while believing that our hectic, frenzied push forward is really an expression of our original creative instincts. But if only creativity were involved we would not be looking for fame and fortune; we would seek guidelines in the expectations of others but would be faithful solely to the directions of our inward power.[3]

Paul was a keeper of the law. He wrote in the letter to the Galatians, "I advanced in Judaism beyond many of my own age . . . so extremely zealous was I for the traditions of my fathers" (Gal. 1:14). The keeping of the law was ultimately to earn the favor of God. This was Paul's motivation, and he set out to destroy the church because he thought this would please God. Paul indicated his dedication to this task by saying that he "persecuted the church of God violently" (v. 13). "Violently" means "to an extraordinary degree," "beyond measure," "utterly." He dedicated himself to earning God's favor by protecting the traditions of his fathers.

What is the motivation for that which is most important in your life at this moment? Is it a deep-down motivation to earn love? If so, your condition is somewhat like that of the apostle Paul when he was trying to please God in order to gain love.

However, such work toward the end of being loved never fills up the need to be loved. Erich Fromm said that

> to be loved because of one's merit, because one deserves it, always leaves doubt; maybe I did not please the person whom I want to love me, maybe this, or that—there is always a fear that love could disappear. Furthermore, 'deserved' love easily leaves a bitter feeling that one is not loved for oneself, that one is loved *only* because one pleases, that one is, in the last analysis, not loved at all but used."[4]

Paul was on this treadmill, grinding out what he thought was his own righteousness which would earn God's favor. Trying to earn love is a debilitating life-style. It requires a person's energies, energies which are spent of oneself for oneself. The kind of favor which this earns does not meet the need for love. It is as a famished person who only gets a few crumbs of food now and then.

What happened to Paul, this little man who was so zealous for earning the favor of God? He discovered, first of all, that he was persecuting the "church of God" and trying "to destroy it" (Gal. 1:13). He encountered the living Christ, near Damascus, who asked him, "Why do you persecute me?" (Acts 9:4).

Surprising, isn't it? How could Paul persecute Christ? Was not Paul persecuting those Christians? He had not seen Christ among any of those who had been the target of his cause. Yet, it was true. Paul later understood that the church was the "body of Christ" (1 Cor. 12:27). Christ is in the church and the church is in Christ. Christ and His church are one. That point of identification is real. If Paul had a Christian whipped, Christ was whipped. When Paul threw someone into prison, he imprisoned Christ. Christ suffered because of Paul.

Not only are the church and Christ one, but also God and Christ are one. To persecute the church means to persecute Christ, and to persecute Christ means to throw yourself against

God. The encounter with Christ on the road to Damascus awakened Paul to these truths.

Paul made a terrible mistake. He tried to please God, and
thought he did please God, by attacking the church. He discovered that the church he was battling was God's church, and that
God's Son so identified with His people, His church, that Paul
actually had attacked the very Son of God Himself! For one who
had set out to please God, Paul had gone completely in the
wrong direction. He had done the opposite of his intention—he
set himself against God with all the zeal he could muster.

Attempting to earn love can take some wrong directions and
prove to be costly. For the executive with a driving need for
approval (love), the cost may be ulcers and emotional exhaus-
tion. Seeking to earn love may be an energy-draining attempt
to save his own life. The homemaker may experience lonely
tension-filled frustration, for fear of not being loved is a lonely,
frustrating experience. For the young person, the effort may
lead to unhealthy compromise, for a person may even sacrifice
her potential and ethics in order to be accepted (loved).

Emotional burnout, or emotional overheating, occurs when
people live in fear of a sense of ultimate rejection if they cannot
earn love in some way. Efforts to earn love may build rather
meaningless relationships. It is a mistake to live life outwardly
with a price tag on it as, "I am pretending to love you so that
you will love me." That is a manipulating kind of antilove. It
benefits neither the person giving it nor the one receiving it.
This kind of outgoing life is counterproductive.

The Gift of Love

What happened to Paul who, while trying to earn the favor
of God, discovered that he had made this mistake of setting
himself against God? Did God strike him with a lightning bolt?
Drive him six feet under with a mallet? Suck him under in the
crevices of an earthquake? Flog him to death with a tree? Paul

could have said in response, "I deserve it all, for I set myself against the church of God."

But Paul did not get what he deserved. Jesus did not destroy him in that encounter near Damascus. Christ loved him just at the point when Paul was as far removed from God as he could be. When he was utterly alienated from God, Paul discovered that he was not annihilated but loved.

And what kind of love was it? *Eros?* Did God say to Paul, "Now I am going to get even with you. You have been against Me. Now I am going to use you for My benefit. I am going to get some good out of you. You are so much of an object, and I will throw you away as a person would an oil filter once it has served its purpose."

Was it a limited kind of *philos* love? Did God say, "I will be friendly to you if you will be friendly to Me. You may be included in our group if you shape up and act right from now on. But if one mistake happens again, then you are out!"

It was *agape* love. God reached out and enclosed Paul with His loving acceptance, treating him as one of dignity and value.

Invited to a neighboring church for the dedication of a new building, I went with the idea of finding a seat among the congregation and participating in the service. The service was already in progress when I arrived. However, when I walked into the building, movements occurred on the platform as several people changed chairs. Then someone came to me and ushered me to the platform and gave me the seat in the center of the platform!

How did I feel? I felt honored. I felt somewhat overwhelmed by the gracious acceptance I received. The place of honor was given to me not because of merit, but because of the grace of that church and its leaders. I had done nothing to help with the new building.

What if, however, I had gone to the church as an enemy, one who had done everything he could to keep the new building from happening? What if I had persecuted the church, convinced the local authorities to put the leaders in jail, and even encouraged the stoning of the building and the people while they were at worship? While I had not deserved the honored treatment I received from the church when I came as a friend, I certainly would not have deserved the gracious acceptance if I had come as an enemy. I would have deserved to have myself locked away, tried, and sentenced to imprisonment for persecuting that church.

Even when Paul had done only harm to the church, Christ received him and gave him a place of honor. A person who had been an archenemy was accepted as a friend. Oh, Christ did not begin to love him when Paul became a friend; Christ loved Paul when he was an enemy. Paul spoke out of personal experience when he said, "God shows his love for us in that while we were yet sinners Christ died for us" (Rom. 5:8). Christ died for those who were totally alienated from Him. Paul knew that he was that sinner. Just when he was at the point of being God's greatest enemy, that was the point at which Paul discovered that he was loved and accepted by God. Such love cannot be earned; it is a gift.

All of us need to understand that the same gift is ours. We do not have to earn love, we already are loved. All of us need this unconditional, unlimited love of God. Eric Fromm said, "Unconditional love corresponds to one of the deepest longings . . . of every human being."[5] That love is already extended by God. One only has to accept it.

Reaching the Sinner

Some people feel that eternal punishment should be the major emphasis of preaching. Messages of doom, destruction, and threats should resound often from the pulpit, they claim. Warn them of sin and hell. Frighten them—that is the only way to get to them.

Sin sometimes is defined as "missing the mark." This means to me that I have missed the mark as to who I really am. Sin is a failure to be who we are. Who are we? We are God's children, created and sustained and loved by Him in Jesus Christ. We are of value and dignity. God gifted us with the potential to be truly human and belong to Him. People who are not in relationship to Him are lost from their true identity, their potential as human beings, and their destiny.

People do need to be warned about this abysmal lostness and the consequences, which means eternal death unless something is done. At the same time, however, playing upon people's guilt and fear should not be used as a means of driving them to God. There are at least two reasons for objecting to such a practice.

In the first place, a relationship based upon the fear, guilt, or both is wrong. A relationship consisting of fear and guilt from the human side is a prison, a prison from which there is a deep-seated desire to escape. Friendship is impossible when a person attempts to relate to another human being out of fear or guilt. A marriage could not exist in such a relationship; indeed, neither can real relationship with God.

People who attempt to be loyal to God out of fear or guilt would escape if they could. However, they feel that God holds the power and calls all the shots. There is no point in trying to escape. God is bigger than they, so they don't stand a chance. The only choice, they think, is to go on fearing God and bearing guilt so that He will let them into heaven. If they do not, eternal death is their only option. Or, as Dorothy Sayers wrote, "The God of Christians is too often looked upon as an old gentleman of irritable nerves who beats people for whistling."[6] That view of God is unattractive and unattracting.

In the second place, God does not come at us with weapons of fear and guilt in order to manipulate us into doing His will. He acts upon us with love, because His way with us is the way of love. In fact, He wants to remove fear and guilt and free us to be a real human beings, to find our own identity, and to chart our destiny toward heaven.

Wallace Hamilton, a Methodist preacher, recorded a beautiful story told to him by G. W. Rosenberry. Rosenberry, traveling on a train, noticed that a young man near him seemed to be nervous and upset. As a minister, he offered his services to the young man, who then told his story. The young man and his father had argued. Words were said, and the young man left home in anger and rebellion. Now he was returning, and he had sent word to his folks that he would be passing the house on this train at this time of day. He further instructed them that if they wanted him to stay to hang something white in front of the house. If he saw nothing white, then he would continue on the train and not bother them anymore.

As they rounded a curve in the tracks near the young man's home, what they saw caused them both to become excited. Everywhere they looked they could see white—the house, the barn, the trees were covered in white. It seems that the father and mother had taken every white sheet, tablecloth, and pillowcase they could find and had hung them out in order to welcome home their wayward son. God comes to us like that with His abundant love and acceptance.[7]

God, in His loving, redeeming action upon us causes us to fling ourselves into His arms. I have found that most sinners already know they are sinners and are in trouble. They simply have accepted alienation from God as a way of life, if indeed they believe God exists. Most people need to be made aware of the loving, accepting Father who already has accepted and loved them.

The people to whom Jesus gave warning and spoke judgment were the religionists, not the publicans and sinners. The publicans and sinners flocked to Jesus—to hear Him, to touch Him. They were drawn by His acceptance, His compassion, and His words of truth, which were all expressions of *agapē*.

A young couple felt alienated from God by their failures. They were uncomfortable about a visit from the minister, for they were certain they would hear judgment and condemnation once they confessed their sins. They were grateful that he could listen to their sins and failures with sympathy and tell them that Jesus wanted them and loved them still. (I often have seen the relief from grief and pain show in the faces of people when, after confessing their sins, they were assured that God had not rejected them but still loved them as much as He always did.)

After all, isn't that the way Jesus received us and reacted to us? That is the way Paul was received. Oh, he knew he was a sinner. We knew that we had greatly missed the mark ourselves, but we have encountered God's love in Christ. This couple knew they had alienated themselves from God, yet the love of Christ was still there for their receiving. God acts upon our lives, as He did in Paul's life, with *agapē*.

We should accept that God loves us. Jesus told His disciples that they were salt and light (Matt. 5:13-14). He did not say, "You shall become salt," or "You shall become light." We already *are* salt and light. We don't need to pretend that we are not, for such salt loses its "taste" (v. 13). We do not need to hide the fact that we are light, for that is senseless as well as suppressive.

It would be strange—contradictory and funny—if we saw a lump of salt going about saying, "I am not a lump of salt," or a lightening bolt going about saying, "I am not light." We laugh at comedy skits in which a policeman, fully uniformed and having forgotten he is a policeman, runs frantically about calling for a policeman. We are already loved. Can we accept ourselves as being loved unconditionally by the Father?

Scientists say this cosmos has been in existence for thirteen billion years and that our earth is only a speck of dust in comparison with the Milky Way. The Milky Way has at least a hundred billion individual stars, our sun being one among them. On top of that, the Milky Way is only a speck of dust compared with the galactic clusters, some containing ten thousand galaxies, which means that the number of observable galaxies is approximately one hundred million.[8] Staggering, isn't it? Yet the amazing thing about all this created splendor and creative power of God is that each human being is the focal point of it all. The ultimate aim of all this creative work is the human being. And what is the content and character of the creative focus of God? It is *agapē*.

Love and Change

The result of that Creative Power whose content is *agapē*, focused upon a responsive individual, is a changed person. In fact, Paul emphasized that "if any one is in Christ, he is a new creation" (2 Cor. 5:17). Paul was speaking out of his personal experience, because his encounter with Christ who loved him made him a new person. The word "creation" almost certainly points back to the creation account in the first chapter of Genesis. It is a reference to the power of God in bringing creation into being. That same Power which called into existence the stars, the sun, the earth, the moon—in short, the universe—was the Power which made Paul into a new creation. Now what was the content, the character, of that Creative Power? Paul would have said, "love," *agapē*. Paul spoke of the "Son of God, who loved me and gave himself for me" (Gal. 2:20).

So, Saul who was a persecutor became Paul an apostle. He spoke of this radical change in 1 Corinthians 15:8, as he called himself one who was "untimely born." This expression refers to a sudden and violent transition from one existence to another, as a baby born prematurely. Paul was torn from his previous course of life by the loving, transforming acceptance of God and set on a whole new course of experience.

If Paul the persecutor can be changed into an apostle by the invading love of God, so can we be changed. We can be changed from small, self-seeking beings to those who are others-centered and growing into real human beings. We can be changed from thinking of ourselves as worthless to those who think of ourselves as valuable, for if the mighty God loves us, are we not valuable? We can be changed from lostness, as Paul was when he was persecuting the church, to life, which he found in the new relationship of love in Jesus Christ. To be loved by the Creator, simply because I am, is a life-filling experience. That is *agapē.* That is the supreme life of love acting upon our lives.

One of the religious classics is the *Varieties of Religious Experience* by William James, a book composed of lectures delivered originally in 1901-1902. A great part of the book is devoted to the study of conversion experiences and effects of the conversion to faith in God. "One of the commonest entries in conversion records" which James noted was the sense of "newness within and without." James used Jonathan Edwards' recounting of his experience to illustrate:

> After this my sense of divine things gradually increased, and became more and more lively, and had more of that inward sweetness. The appearance of everything was altered; there seemed to be, as it were, a calm, sweet cast, or appearance of divine glory, in almost everything. God's excellency, His wisdom, His purity and love, seemed to appear in everything; in the sun, moon, and stars; in the clouds and blue sky; in the grass, flowers, and trees; in the water and all nature; which used greatly to fix my mind. And scarce anything, among all the works of nature, was so sweet to me as thunder and lightning; formerly nothing had been so terrible to me. Before, I used to be uncommonly terrified with thunder, and to be struck with terror when I saw a thunderstorm rising; but now, on the contrary, it rejoices me.[9]

Jonathan Edwards was a new man in a new world. So was the apostle Paul. So have countless others become as they have accepted God who acts upon every individual with *agapē.* God's *agapē,* seen and accepted in His son Jesus Christ, is the way of change.

Notes

1. Anders Nygren, *Agape and Eros,* trans. by Philip S. Watson, 1st rev. ed. (London: S.P.C.K., 1953) p. 112.

2. Joseph Simone and James Reidy, *The Risk of Loving* (New York: The Seabury Press, 1973), p. 61.

3. Ibid., pp. 61-62.

4. Erich Fromm, *The Art of Loving* (New York: Bantam Books, 1963) p. 35.

5. Ibid.

6. Dorthy Sayers, *The Mind of the Maker* (San Francisco: Harper & Row, 1941), p. 12.

7. Wallace Hamilton, *Horns and Halos in Human Nature* (Westwood, N.J.: Fleming H. Revell Company, 1954), pp. 150-151.

8. Hans Kung, *Does God Exist?* trans., by Edward Quinn (New York: Doubleday & Company, 1980), pp. 640-641.

9. William James, *The Varieties of Religious Experience* (The Fontana Library of Theology and Philosophy, 1974), p. 248.

4

Love and Need for Community

When His visible Presence was withdrawn from men's sight, what was left as the fruit of His Ministry? Not a formulated creed, not a body of writings in which a new philosophy of life was expounded, but a group of men and women who found themselves knit together in a fellowship closer than any that they had known, and who became the nucleus of the whole Christian Church. (William Temple).[1]

Loneliness is the most difficult thing I have to deal with (An elder friend).

God shows his love for us (Rom. 5:8).

In his book, *Why Am I Afraid to Love?* John Powell told the story of Mike Gold.[2] Communism had gained some popularity in this country in the 1920s, and Mike Gold was American Communism's philosopher. Soon, however, Communism fell into disrepute and Mike Gold became an unknown. In his solitude he wrote about his experiences. In telling of his childhood, he said his mother instructed him to never wander out of the area bounded by four certain streets. She did not tell him that he was in a Jewish ghetto and that the prejudices he would experience beyond those four streets would harm him. One day, however, his curiosity led him out of his boundaries. Some older boys accosted him, accused him of being a Christ-killer, of whom he had never heard, and beat him terribly.

Mike Gold died in New York in 1967. The last meals he had were taken in a Catholic charity house.

What if, beyond those boundaries that his mother had set for him, Mike Gold had encountered acceptance and affirmation instead of the rejection and abuse. What if, instead of calling him a "Christ-killer," those boys had communicated to him in some way the love of Christ? Had Gold experienced community and acceptance in the Spirit of Christ, his life may have been altogether more positive and happy.

Community, A Basic Need

We are made for relationships. In the very beginning, God said, "It is not good that the man should be alone" (Gen. 2:18). It is not good for any person to be alone.

Relationships can be negative. Wherever community is governed by the self-interest of those who make it up, the impact upon the members of that community is negative. Anger, suspicion, competition, unhappiness, and, ultimately, rejection exist. Obviously, such community is more an anticommunity than anything else.

Sin is destructive, and it manifests itself primarily in the destruction of community. Consider the account of Adam and Eve again. Community, or communion, in the beginning existed between God and persons and persons with one another. The result of the disobedience of Adam and Eve was the disruption of that community. Dietrich Bonhoeffer said of this event,

> Whereas the primal relationship of man to man is a giving one, in the state of sin it is purely demanding. Every man exists in a state of complete voluntary isolation; each man lives his own life, instead of all living the same God-life.[3]

Bonhoeffer was right. After the disruption of community by Adam and Eve, Cain got into the act. His self-interest, expressed in jealousy and suspicion, led him to kill his brother. Rather than building community, he destroyed community.

The Bible tells it like it is. Nation sets itself against nation, family against family, person against person. The destruction of community happens over and over again, and such destruction is sinful.

Of course, the situation is very serious today. Our self-interest takes precedence over our interest in our neighbor. As a result, although we need one another, we build walls between ourselves and everyone suffers. Henri J. M. Nouwen wrote,

> Loneliness is one of the most universal sources of human suffering today. Psychiatrists and clinical psychologists speak about it as the most frequently expressed complaint and the root not only of an increasing number of suicides but also of alcoholism, drug use, different psychosomatic symptoms—such as, headaches, stomach and low back pains—and a large number of traffic accidents.[4]

Nouwen further stated that "we are living in a world where the most intimate relationships have become a part of competition and rivalry." Nouwen named pornography as one of the results of the lack of relationships. He said, "It is intimacy for sale." Lonely people, who have no meaningful community with others, will look for substitutes. They are the victims of their own failure to be a community to someone else. Self-centeredness wants community that feeds self, and that community is self-destructive. So relationships are approached on the basis of, "What's in this relationship for me?" rather than, "How can I build a meaningful, responsible relationship with another?" Relationships are superficial and cheap, and although community may appear to exist, it doesn't.

What happens to community when self-centered interest enters may be illustrated in a story.[5] A merchant in the Midwest had identical twin sons. The two were inseparable as they grew. They dressed alike and participated in the same activities. After their father died, they returned to their hometown to run the family business.

One morning, after waiting on a customer, one brother placed a dollar from a sale on the top of the cash register. Later, he remembered that he put the dollar bill there and went to place it in the cash register. However, it was gone.

He asked his twin about it, who said he knew nothing of the dollar bill. The first twin indicated that that was strange, because no one had been in the store since the purchase except the two of them.

The first twin did not let the matter drop, but asked his brother again, with a noticeable hint of suspicion in his voice, about the dollar bill. The second twin flared back in anger, and the first breach of trust occurred between them. It was a break that grew wider and wider as accusations and counteraccusations were hurled. Even the community took sides. They dissolved their partnership, and ran a partition through the middle of the store. Each then engaged in angry competition with the other. This state of affairs continued for twenty years.

One day a well-dressed stranger came into the store. He went to one side of the store to inquire of one of the brothers as to how long he had been in business. After being told the length of time, the man indicated that he had an old score to settle.

He explained that twenty years ago he was drifting from place to place. He had gotten off a boxcar in the brothers' town. He had no money, and he had not eaten for three days. He explained that he was walking in the alley behind the store and saw through the open door a dollar bill on the cash register. No one was around to see him as everyone was in front of the store. He had never stolen before, but he was so hungry he submitted to the temptation and took the dollar. He explained that he was now back to make amends and pay what was appropriate for any damages.

When he had finished his story, the stranger was surprised to see the man before him shaking his head and weeping. The stranger was asked to go next door and tell the story to another, and he noticed that the other looked exactly like the first. After

the stranger told his story again, there were two men standing
before him weeping.

That is a sad story. Those two were brothers. They were
meant to share life together. But because of the destruction of
the community which had existed between them by their
mutual suspicion and self-centered anger, they had denied
themselves twenty years of shared, meaningful life together.
What laughter and joy, what comfort and strength, and what
growth and fulfillment they had missed, all because of the disruption of community by self-interest.

It is a sad story today. Wives and husbands, children and
parents, and communities and nations are busy building walls
between themselves and God. Think of what we are denying
ourselves by destroying community rather than creating it. Our
self-centeredness robs us, our sins destroy us by breaking community with God and with one another.

The Re-creation of Community

Salvation should be understood not only in individual terms
but also in terms of community. Since the time when Adam and
Eve broke the primal community with God and eventually with
others, God has been restoring community. God has taken definite steps to restore the community relationship which humanity lost with Him and with each other.

The Old Testament is generally the story of God calling a
community into existence and seeking to shape the people into
the community which He wanted them to be. He called on the
people to love Him with all their heart, their soul, and their
might (Deut. 6:5). God in His love extended Himself toward His
people to establish community with them, and then they had
the opportunity to extend themselves toward Him in order for
the community to be completed. God intended for there to be
a wonderful reciprocal community which would make for harmony and peace. The same kind of reciprocal community was
to be established among themselves out of the character of

community which God made. The Ten Commandments spell out the character of community, beginning with community with God in the first four Commandments and then moving to the right kind of community with each other in the remaining six.

The Israelites certainly understood that they were called into community with God and each other. Eduard Schweizer[6] noted that the Hebrew language does not possess a word for *body* —that is, body in an individual sense. The Hebrew certainly experienced his physical body, but he simply did not dwell upon it as did the Greeks. Perhaps that is quite shocking to us because we Americans are so concerned about our bodies, to which the current physical fitness craze gives evidence. There were several reasons that the Hebrew did not reflect upon his physical self. Primarily, however, it seems that his lack of concern for body resulted from the fact that he thought of his relationship with God and his fellow Hebrews before he thought in terms of himself. In other words, he thought of himself in terms of community first of all. Schweizer put it this way:

> The very word, body may in Greek single out individuals, whereas in Hebrew the distinction between the one and the many is not of first importance, since man, in his dependence on and his responsibility to God, is at the same time seen in his dependence on and his responsibility to his fellowmen, his family, his tribe, his people.[7]

Jesus came creating community in Himself. He gathered around Him twelve disciples and made a community. Everywhere they went, Jesus extended community to others. He called upon people to repent and come into the kingdom of God, which was an invitation to become a part of the new people of God whom Jesus was creating. He opened this community to everyone. The publicans, sinners, and other outcasts flocked to Him because He opened to them the way to God His

Father. "In Christ God was reconciling the world to himself" (2 Cor. 5:19). What is the world but the community of people whom God loved. Does not John 3:16 say, "For God so loved the world that he gave his only Son"? The world is the community of people with whom Jesus Christ wished to establish community by sharing His saving life with them forever.

After His resurrection, Jesus continued to work through His disciples to extend His salvation and, consequently, to extend community. Remember in Acts that the community was gathered in the upper room where communion with God occurred, and that communion was manifested by the presence of God's Spirit. What did the disciples do then but go out as a community to share with the community around them to include others by salvation through faith into the community?

Paul, of course, went about calling communities into existence in Christ. He understood that those saved were supposed to be community. In Ephesians 2:14, Paul told the Gentiles that Christ had "broken down the dividing wall of hostility" and made both Jesus and Gentiles into one. Verse 15 indicates that Christ's purpose was to make "one new man," which means that Christ made one new humanity out of both Jews and Gentiles. Paul, therefore, understood the importance, in fact the necessity, for people to be in community with God and with one another.

We Are to Make Community

Our purpose also is to extend the community we have with God in Christ and with one another. Jesus called us to extend community "unto the least of these" (Matt. 25:31-40). The hungry, the thirsty, the stranger, the naked, the sick, and the prisoner are to be offered community in the name of Christ. It isn't only a matter of giving food, clothing, and so forth, but, most importantly, it is person establishing communion with another person through the meeting of needs. It is community between person and person, or others and others. We are bound up with the community of humanity. This passage reveals that Christ identifies with the community of humanity and especially the needy.

In Christ's view, the common human bond or community was there. Martin Luther understood the bond of humanity with Christ and with each other as revealed in a letter he wrote to his desperately ill friend, Frederick of Saxony. He wrote in September, 1519,

> When . . . I learned . . . that Your Lordship has been afflicted with a grave illness and that Christ has at the same time become ill to you . . . I cannot pretend that I do not hear the voice of Christ crying out to me from Your Lordship's body and flesh saying, "Behold, I am sick." This is so because such evils as illness . . . are not borne by us who are Christians but by Christ himself, our Lord and Savior, in whom we live, even as Christ plainly testifies . . . when he says, "Inasmuch as ye have done it unto one of the least of these my brethren, you have done it unto me."[8]

Luther's insight of his oneness with his suffering brother is remarkable. It is a concept he learned from Christ. Christ called those who responded to Him and followed Him, including both men and women, His "brethren" (Mark 3:34, KJV). The New Testament emphasized that even masters and slaves were brothers and on equal relationship (Philem. 16). Also, Christ called people "from every tribe and tongue and people and nation" (Rev. 5:9) into one community.

We are responsible for making community also. In Romans 14, a conflict between those who were called "strong" and those who were called "weak" is depicted. The "weak" in the conflict seem to be those who had not yet reached the point of spiritual maturity to realize their liberty in Christ from legalistic standards of righteousness. They stressed regulations concerning the eating of certain meats and regulations concerning the observance of certain days as being necessary to following Christ. The "strong" evidently were the more spiritually mature, be-

lieving that the observance of such legalistic measures was unnecessary.

The danger, however, more than the matter of who was theologically correct at that point, was the fact that community was
threatened. Some situations did exist where community was not
possible, as the case with the man living in incest described in
1 Corinthians 5. What he was doing was so alien to the community that he could not be included unless he gave up the sinful
relationship. However, the issue between the weak and the
strong was not an issue which would prevent community. Nevertheless, disruption of community was happening, because
one group was despising the other and the other was judging
the first.

Paul put the burden of responsibility on the strong. They
were the more mature and more stable. They were to be toler-
ant of the weak. If the strong did that which caused the brother
to stumble, they would bring to ruin "one for whom Christ
died" (Rom. 14:15). Rather than doing that, Paul said, "Let us
then pursue what makes for peace and for mutual upbuilding"
(v. 19). And what is "mutual upbuilding" except building up the
community in Christ? Likewise, we are to maintain, strengthen,
and build up the community which we have in Christ and with
one another.

As far as the church in the New Testament is concerned, the
local communities of faith reached out to one another in order
to build relationship. For example, Paul engaged in taking an
offering for Jewish Christians in Palestine during the latter part
of his ministry in the east. One purpose of the offering was to
alleviate the economic distress of the saints at Jerusalem. The
offering, however, had additional significance to that of reliev-
ing the poverty conditions among the Jewish Christians in
Palestine.

A division existed at the time of the collection between the
Jewish Christian churches and the Gentile Christian churches.
The problem was mostly from the Jewish side. Many Jewish

Christian converts had brought over into their Christianity their old Jewish exclusivism and prejudices. Paul planned to use the offering not only to relieve the famine conditions but to break down barriers to community as well. So he made a collection among the Gentile churches to be given to the Jewish churches.

Moreover, Paul planned to deliver the gift himself so that he might serve as a bridge builder between Jewish and Gentile Christians. The Gentile churches extended their community through the offering toward the Jewish churches. They were making and maintaining community beyond the confines of their local communities.

But not only was giving on the part of the Gentiles important, the receiving on the part of the Jewish Christians was vital as well. Community must be extended, but the other person must be willing to receive.

Love, the Basis of Community

Perhaps no community in the New Testament had more difficulty building community than the church at Corinth. The church was almost hopelessly split by groups and problems. James Moffatt described the church as one

> where ascetic difficulties, a women's movement, the inveterate party-spirit of city-life, the Greek passion for rhetoric and theosophy, pietistic ardours, a love for what was showy and exciting, and personal animosities, due in part to differences in culture and social position, were threatening to tear the church asunder.[9]

The truth of the matter is that the Corinthians had not left behind the fragmentation of the world from which they came when they came into the Christian faith. They were a dismembered body, with each part attempting to function apart from the whole. So Paul pointed out the implausibility for such existence when he asked the question, "Is Christ divided?" (1 Cor.

1:13). The obvious answer, of course, was that Christ was not divided. Therefore, it was impossible for the church, which is the body of Christ, to be divided and still exist as the church.

How was the church to be welded together into the oneness of community which God intended for it? Paul told how in chapters 12 through 14 in 1 Corinthians. These chapters form a unit which deal primarily with the problem concerning spiritual gifts (1 Cor. 12:1) and secondarily with all the problems of the church. The pivotal chapter of the three, and really of the whole book, is chapter 13, which is Paul's hymn of love.

Actually, all three chapters are about love and the building of community. The real purpose of the three chapters is to propose love as a solution to the problem causing disunity and the destruction of community. The love theme can be detected in chapter 12. Paul stressed in verse 7 that each spiritual gift was given for the common good. The gifts were not for self-gratification or merely for the spiritual profit of the recipient. In other words, the gifts were for the purpose of building a caring community. J. S. Reuf wrote:

> The opposite of division is care for one another. It is not a situation in which there is mere consensus. The community of faith does not operate on the basis of compromise, but of loving concern. Paul envisages a community in which everyone cares about the other person. This love, which is the highest manifestation of the Spirit at work, is the source of the church's unity.[10]

The implicit theme of love in chapter 12, evidenced by the emphasis upon care for one another and the building of community, becomes explicit in chapter 13. Paul proclaimed love as the more excellent way. It is the way to building community.

Chapter 14 depicts the practical application of love around the theme of prophecy. Prophecy is not foretelling in this context, but speaking forth the will of God to a given situation. One who so speaks puts love into action and builds community (see v. 3). The person who becomes the instrument for communicating God's will acts in the interest of others and for the common good of community.

But what kind of love is it about which Paul spoke? Throughout 1 Corinthians 13, the Greek word translated "love" is *agapē*. We have stressed already that Paul, when writing of love, reserved the noun *agapē* to refer to God's love. So he was thinking in terms of God's love throughout chapters 12 through 14. This is the reason love is said to be greater than faith or hope as Paul said, in verse 13. Faith and hope are human responses to God. Love—*agapē* love—is of divine origin.

The way for the church at Corinth to build real community was by exercising the love they had first experienced from God in Jesus Christ. It is readily understood that if Christians, as members of the body of Christ, exercise toward one another the self-giving love which is God's love, barriers to community will be shattered.

Shantung Compound by Langdon Gilkey is the story of an effort to build a community in a concentration camp. Foreigners in China during World War II were herded into a civilian internment camp by the Japanese military. They were not subjected to tortures as some were in military camps, but some two thousand people had to live together for two-and-a-half years in very crowded, unsanitary conditions. This cross section of humanity, representing religious and secular vocations of all kinds, as well as prostitutes, junkies, and old and young people, had to make themselves into community. Gilkey chronicled the development of the community as they organized themselves and assigned and took responsibilities. At one stage of development the threat of anarchy brought into question the continued existence of the community as a community.

It was at this point that Gilkey said he realized that the survival of any community is dependent upon its moral strength. There must be enough people in the community who operate out of a moral concern for the community as a whole if any community is to survive. Gilkey frankly admitted that at first the only vocation he thought they could not use in the camp was the religious calling. Later he realized that the "many secular vocations and skills the camp needed were of use to us only if the men who performed them had some inner strength." Gilkey stated further that

> the ultimate roots of social law and order extend down to the same moral and religious depths of the self where lies the basis of cooperation and sharing. If a man is committed only to his own survival and advancement, or to that of his family and group, then under pressure, neither will he share with his neighbor nor be obedient to the law. Had our community been made up solely of such men, all cooperative action devoted to the production and distribution of food, and all courts and laws devoted to the maintenance of order would have become inoperative.[11]

Furthermore, Gilkey said that

> sin may be defined as an ultimate religious devotion to a finite interest; it is an overriding loyalty or concern for the self, its existence and its prestige, or for the existence and prestige of a group. From this deeper sin, that is, from this inordinate love of the self and its own, stem the moral evils of indifference, injustice, prejudice, and cruelty to one's neighbor, and the other destructive patterns of action that we call "sins."[12]

People are good many times without being believers in God. Enough moral strength exists in such goodness to have community. Community in such a case, although better than no community, has limitations. It tends to operate out of the *philia*-type love, which is love for a friend. This is a good love, but as established in the first chapter of this book, this love can be narrow, for it chooses to love its kind, or its group, or its race unless it is motivated by and built upon *agapē* love.

For community to exist at its best, let it be dominated and motivated by *agapē* love. It is the "more excellent way" (1 Cor. 12:31). It is self-giving. It is expended life in behalf of others and oneself in order to build the life of all.

The remarkable thing about this love, where it is truly expressed, is that no barriers exist. This kind of love even opens community to the enemy. When Jesus instructed that his followers were to love their enemies, he was not speaking of loving them at a distance. To love one's enemy means to seek to establish relationship with him in the love of Christ, to even serve the enemy and work for his welfare.

Love, the Bond of Perfection

The church is to be the community of faith which exercises outwardly the love with which it has been loved by God. God's love is the glue that holds the community together and enables the community to extend itself even to the enemy, because "God shows his love for us in that while we were yet sinners Christ died for us" (Rom. 5:8). The church should aspire to extend community on the basis of that kind of love. Of course, we have not arrived in this matter—sometimes we love with that love as local churches, as communities of God, and sometimes we do not. Nevertheless, such love should be our goal.

Paul saw love as the "bond" which perfects community. In fact, the reference occurs in a context where Paul instructed the Colossian Christians to put on several things—"kindness, lowliness, meekness, and patience" (Col. 3:12). Then he instructed them in verse 14 to "put on love, which binds everything together in perfect harmony" (Col. 3:14).

It is God's kind of love, *agapē*, which must be put on. As the church puts on love, it puts on that which makes it most like its Creator. In putting on love the church is being true to its nature as the people of God. Also, as the church puts on love, it is putting on that which makes for perfect harmony in the body of Christ. Therefore, community is built and others are included into the community.

The world, and you and I, desperately need this community of love. How different Mike Gold's life might have been had he met such a church. How much richer your neighbor's life, or your son's, your daughter's, your mother's, or father's life might be if you extend to them community which arises out of the love of God. As we seek to extend community in love, we are engaging in the work of God, for God extends community to us. He does because He is love and His way with us is the way of love.

Notes

1. William Temple, *Christian Faith and Life* (London: SCM Press LTD, 1963), p. 127.

2. John Powell, *Why Am I Afraid to Love?* (Niles, Ill.: Argus Communications, 1972), pp. 114-116.

3. Dietrich Bonhoeffer, *Sanctorium Communio,* trans. and rev. by R. Gregory Smith (London: Collins 1963), p. 71.

4. Henri J. M. Nouwen, *Reaching Out: The Three Movements of the Spiritual Life* (New York: Doubleday and Company, Inc., 1975), p. 15.

5. John Claypool, *The Preaching Event* (Waco, Tex.: Word Books, 1980), pp. 37-39.

6. Eduard Schweizer, *The Church as the Body of Christ* (Richmond, Va.: John Knox Press, 1964), p. 17.

7. *Ibid.,* p. 19.

8. Martin Luther, *Letters of Spiritual Counsel,* ed. by Theodore G. Tapper (Philadelphia: The Westminster Press, 1955), p. 27.

9. James Moffatt, *Love in the New Testament* (London: Hodder and Straughton, 1919), p. 182.

10. J. S. Ruef, *Paul's First Letter to Corinth,* The Pelican New Testament Commentaries, ed. by Dennis Nineham (Baltimore: Penguin Books, 1971), p. 136.

11. Langdon Gilkey, *Shantung Compound* (New York: Harper & Row, 1966), p. 161.

12. *Ibid.* p. 233.

5

Love and Evil

Whether the philosopher be atheist or Christian, he is living in a universe in which he has to try to make sense not only of the mystery of the relation of time to eternity, but also the problem of the co-existence of good and evil. (Leonard Hodgson).[1]

Why does God allow evil in this world if He really cares for us? (A church member).

God shows his love for us (Rom. 5:8).

It was difficult to see him, lying as he was in a crumpled heap on the narrow shoulder of the highway, so we almost passed him by. Several cars stopped. After being helped to his feet, and after having awakened somewhat from his drunken stupor, he told his story. He had been paid his wages at the end of the workday the evening before. He met some friends at the bar that evening, and they induced him to drink heavily. After he was sufficiently drunk, his "friends" got him in a car, took his money, and dumped him on the isolated stretch of highway which ran through the swamp.

The scene of the crumpled figure lying beside the highway impressed itself upon my mind as a parable of the consequences of evil. He was in danger, exposed to the elements, as well as to the vehicles rushing by. Evil brings us into danger in what otherwise may be friendly surroundings. He was robbed of his resources. Indeed, I wondered if the crumpled figure had enough strength to stand up by himself. Evil robs us of our resources also; everything that is important to us can be lost to evil. He was alone. No friends or family were with him, only strangers standing by at whom he blinked in confusion. Evil unchecked ultimately leaves one alone.

And there was pain, a pain of the soul lined into his face. Always evil brings its pain. We have seen it in the anguished faces of war-battered mothers and children and brutalized families. We know and see the pain inflicted upon the innocent and the guilty by others. And what is pain except, as C. S. Lewis said, "unmasked, unmistakable evil."[2]

Where does God in His love fit into this situation? Yet there is a still deeper question: Why does God who is love allow the existence of evil in the first place? How did evil get into a world created by One who is love? Was there some mistake? Did God sneeze as He painted this world into existence and mar the painting with His brush?

A Good World

My son was only four years old at the time, but he had an answer to a big question which was puzzling him. The day before we had discovered a snake in our backyard. We took that opportunity to teach him of the danger of snakes. He had been trying to put in some perspective the fact that a mean snake could inject itself into his rather lovely world. "Dad," he said, "I've got it figured out; a good God created the world and a bad god created snakes." That was his explanation for the origin and presence of evil as he perceived it in a snake. Even at that age, he recognized that a good God and evil did not belong together.

Unknown to my son, almost two thousand years before a group in Colossae had come to something of the same answer, except their view was more radical. They were called *Gnostics*. The Gnostics' philosophy was not completely developed at the time Paul wrote his Letter to the Colossians, but some basic beliefs of their world view were present already. They believed all matter was evil, even the human body. Only a divine spark locked away in an individual was good. The divine spark could be directed back to its origin, the good God, if a person had the right *gnōsis,* which is the Greek word for knowledge and the word from which their name, Gnostics, was derived.

They believed that the world was evil and that it had been created that way. The good God put out a being, according to their view, slightly inferior to God but worthy of having come from Him. That being put out another being slightly inferior to itself, and so on down the line with each of the beings inferior to the one before until a completely evil being was created. This evil being, or evil god, created the world, which meant that the world was evil in every aspect because its creator was evil.

Paul reacted strongly against that view, especially in Colossians 1:15-20. Paul said, in effect, that this is a good world made by a good Creator. It is good because Jesus was the agent in creation (v. 16). Three very important prepositional phrases clamor for our attention in verse 16. The creation occurred *in* Christ, *through* Christ, and *for* Christ. Also, Paul said that "all the fulness of God was pleased to dwell" in Christ (v. 19). Therefore, the God who expressed Himself in Jesus Christ is the same God who created the universe. The character and nature of God who revealed Himself fully in Christ is the same as the One who created.

What is that character and nature? Is evil present? Even a casual reading of Matthew, Mark, Luke, or John reveals that there was no evil in Christ. God came in Christ to "preach good news to the poor . . . , to proclaim release to the captives and recovering of sight to the blind, to set at liberty those who are oppressed" (Luke 4:18-19). He touched the untouchables; He accepted the outcasts and forgave them; He even loved those who crucified Him, extending to them the forgiveness of God.

Never do we see evil in the Christ of the New Testament. If Christ is the expression of the character and nature of God— and He is—we know that God is incapable of evil because evil is not a part of His nature. God, then, could not be the source of evil in this world. God created a world without evil.

However, not everyone agrees with this conclusion. Some believe that God is all-powerful, but not all good. God is good, but He has a dark side to His nature, they reason, because if God were both all-powerful and good no evil would exist. So, God must have imperfections and failures bound up with His goodness. John Roth, for example, advances the view that nobody is completely OK, not even God. God has allowed His will to be violated or He has left undone goodness which He could have done. Roth quoted the modern author Camus as being correct that "man is not entirely to blame; it was not he who started history." Roth believes that God exists, but He exists as the God in whom both good and bad are bound up together.[3]

Some take the view that God has a dark side to His nature to extreme ends. God, for example, was both in a Jewish boy who was hanged and also in the German guards who hanged him. God suffered in the boy, but He also acted in the guards. Such is the dark side of the nature of God, according to such a view. This view is not simplistic; it is an involved and detailed argument. It is an attempt to explain the paradox of the coexistence of an all-powerful God and the reality of evil.

However, I rebel at the suggestion that God has a dark side. I do so primarily because of Jesus Christ. I believe fully that God was in Christ reconciling the world to Himself. I believe that Jesus reveals who God is and what God is like. He is, for example, like the father who loves his children. He is like the shepherd who will go and search for the one lost sheep (Luke 15:3-7). He is One who gives all of Himself in His Son to die on the cross. God is good. God is love. God is self-giving love as we have established already. There is no darkness in God.

The view that God has a dark side to His nature which is tied up with the existence of evil is a radical view. There are two other approaches which represent more the major mainstreams of thought as one tries to explain the existence of evil in a world created by a good and all-powerful God. One is called the Irena-ean view. It is named after the early Christian Irenaeus (AD 120-202). He, along with other Greek-speaking writers of that period, developed a view of the existence of evil in this world.

Their approach proposed a two-stage development in the creation of humankind. In the first step of development, human beings became intelligent, ethical, and religious animals. This means they were created in the "image of God." However, they were created as spiritually and morally immature creatures. A long process of further growth and development, in which human beings respond with their free choices, has been taking place since then. In this process, human beings are being brought into the "likeness of God," which is the second stage of development.[4]

John Hick, in a modern interpretation of this view, gave the following summary:

> (1) The divine intention in relation to humankind, according to our hypothesis, is to create perfect finite personal beings in filial relationship with their Maker.
>
> (2) It is logically impossible for humans to be created already in this perfect state, because in its spiritual aspect it involves coming freely to an uncoerced consciousness of God from a situation of epistemic distance, and in its moral aspect, freely choosing the good in preference to evil.
>
> (3) Accordingly the human being was initially created through the evolutionary process, as a spiritually and morally immature creature, and as part of a world which is both religiously ambiguous and ethically demanding.
>
> (4) Thus that one is morally imperfect (i.e., that there is moral evil), and that the world is a challenging and even dangerous environment (i.e., that there is natural evil), are necessary aspects of the present stage of the process through which God is gradually creating perfected finite persons.[5]

Hick views the fall of humanity in chapter 3 of Genesis as depicting the immense difference between what humanity is and what God intends humanity to be. Humanity was created at a distance from God, rather than in perfect closeness to God, so that human beings by free choice could come to know, love, and respond to their Maker. It was necessary to create human beings as immature, and in a somewhat hostile environment, so that moral growth and development could occur. Evil arises out of human imperfection and moral immaturity as wrong choices are made, by individual and corporate humanity, in responding to a challenging and hostile environment.[6]

A second major approach to the problem of evil is that advocated first by Augustine (AD 354-430). Augustine said that God originally created a world in which no moral and natural evil existed. In addition, God created human beings who were rational beings with the freedom to choose to obey and love God. Human beings, specifically Adam and Eve, made the wrong choices and evil entered the world and the human situation. Natural evil—destructive events of nature, for example— Augustine attributed to Satan and his forces. Consequently, natural evil is the result of the action of nonhuman spirits.[7]

The Augustinian explanation of the origin of evil, that of free will of both human and nonhuman spirits being exercised wrongly, has been something of a majority position among those attempting to explain the origin and presence of evil. Even the best explanation, however, does not answer all the questions.

In contrasting the two major views, the primary difference is that of the state of human beings in their initial creation. The Irenaean view says that human beings were created as spiritually and morally inmature and not in perfect relationship and harmony with God. The Augustinian view believes that human beings began in perfect relationship and harmony and fell by their wrong choices from that position of harmony into disharmony. The Irenaean view also has an optimistic view of the evolutionary spiritual development of humankind while the Augustinian view is not so optimistic. Interpreters following one view or the other differ in explanation and in some details in each view. Both views have called the Genesis account as well as other biblical revelation to their support.

A World Out of Shape

It is obvious, whatever explanation is given, that much of the world as we know it now is not good nor in harmony with itself nor with God. Again, some people would blame God. I reject that God has a dark side to His nature which expresses evil. This is contrary, to me, to the revelation of Himself in Jesus Christ. God's way with us is the way of *agapē*.

Others attempt to blame the serpent, or Satan. However, even the Genesis account of the fall of Adam and Eve will not support this view.

The Genesis account, interestingly enough, does not explain the origin of evil. The serpent is there, unexplained as to origin. Jesus never attempted to explain the origin of evil. Neither does the rest of the New Testament. John's Gospel talks about the darkness, which was a reference to evil, but he did not explain how darkness came to be. To what point, then, does the Genesis account lead us?

God created Adam and Eve, and placed them in the garden of Eden. The garden of Eden means that God put His human beings into harmonious circumstances. In other words, they were in harmony with God and God's creation. They had the potential to grow and develop without the restriction of previous wrong choices or evil experiences.

However, this primeval potential to be and become was disrupted. Eve was tempted by the serpent to disobey God. She did. Adam was tempted to do the same, and he did. Evil entered the situation, and the harmony that existed between humanity and God and between humanity and creation was disrupted. As the Genesis account indicates, problems for them and for God's creation began at this point.

Notice that the serpent was only the tempter (see Gen. 3:1-7).

As long as Adam and Eve were obedient, the primeval harmony was not disturbed. The presence of the serpent indicates that the temptation comes from without. The temptation indicates that Adam and Eve had a choice.

When God created humanity, He gave human beings the freedom of choice. He did so because He wanted us to be completely free. If we did not have the freedom to choose, we would be puppets controlled by the strings of whatever way God programmed us. God did not want us to be puppets. It was an act of His grace that we were created with freedom to choose.

Unfortunately, Adam and Eve chose to disobey God. At that moment sin entered their human situation, their environment, and disrupted their lives. Therefore, the Genesis account places the problem of evil in this world not with Satan, but with people. In the various views of the origin of evil, except those who would blame God or the devil, the responsibility for the presence of evil is placed at the door of humanity. Human beings push the world out of shape.

Personal Responsibility

May we say, then, that Adam and Eve are the originators of sin? No, not Adam and Eve alone, for all are responsible. The history of Adam and Eve is the history of humanity. We disrupt our own personal harmony by choosing to be disobedient to God. Insofar as we embrace the evil, we become a part of the problem. We add our force of wrong choices to the context. Ultimately, then, we human beings are responsible for the presence and power of evil in this world.

Jesus emphasized that the problem lies in the heart of an individual. By "heart" he was not referring to the organ pumping blood nor only to the emotions. The "heart" was considered to be the person, a designation for the person's intellect, will, and emotions. Disobedient attitudes and choices are the seedbed for sinful acts (Matt. 5:21-48). What comes out of the depths of a person's being defiles him (Mark 7:21-23).

James echoed Christ when he wrote: "Each person is tempted when he is lured and enticed by his own desire. Then desire when it has conceived gives birth to sin; and sin, when it is full-grown brings forth death" (Jas. 1:14-15). Paul wrote to the Colossians that they "once were estranged and hostile in mind, doing evil deeds" until Christ reconciled them and removed the estrangement (Col. 1:21-22). People are responsible for their sins, and the blame can be placed nowhere else.

I have heard people say in reference to sin, "The devil made me do it." Or they might say, "Satan has gotten hold of Jim and is ruining his life." However, Adam and Eve were not forced to do anything wrong. They *chose* to do the wrong. Jesus, and James and Paul after Him, emphasized the personal responsibility we have for our own sin. Satan, tempter, devil, the evil one—or however you may name the force of evil in this world— has no power over us personally, except what we allow. The devil does not ruin Jim's life, Jim does it by his own choice by giving his life over to evil. Just as Adam and Eve chose, we choose. The world out of shape, with all its hurts and anxieties, is humanity's doing. The misshapen world depicts what humanity has done with God's harmony.

Our disruption of the harmony is a betrayal of God's trust, or love. It is the nature of unselfish love that it trusts the other with oneself as well as with what one has. God trusted us with His nature, with Himself, which is one application of our being made in the image of God. He also trusted us with His world. What has humanity as a whole done? At times we have acted correctly. We have been good stewards of His trust. But, also, we have betrayed His nature. We have chosen evil many times when we have acted contrary to what is moral—contrary to what fits us and the creation around us. We have introduced that which is destructive into the love and goodness context in which we were created and in which we are now.

In creating us as free human beings, God gave us much power. He did not leave us powerless when we were placed in dominion over His creation (see Ps. 8). Otherwise, there would be no possibility of having the dominion God called us to have (Gen. 1:28). Human power has love as its content when it is under the sovereignty of God. That same power, however, can be perverted and turned in a destructive direction. The destructive power of evil in this world is overwhelming. We have twisted our power to have dominion in this created order to the invention and manufacture of weapons which can destroy civilization.

Yet, we continue to flirt with evil as if it is nothing. An evil step may be a small one at first, but one tiny decision leads to another, and so the evil grows. Cain, jealous and hateful toward his brother, Abel, finally killed him. Look how that act has multiplied, until brothers and sisters have killed millions of their brothers and sisters. And now, we are posed to wipe out one another completely. This misshapen world depicts how humankind has betrayed God's trust and misused His power.

Unfortunately, our children have to deal with this world gone awry from the moment they arrive, as we did when we were born. They sometimes suffer innocently as we have and do sometimes suffer innocently. That is the nature of sin—it always brings its suffering.

"But," one might ask, "what sin opened the way for cancer's terrible destruction?" Perhaps many things. We do not know the answer to that question. Perhaps we will be better able to give an answer in years ahead. Who knows what human willfulness might have upset creation's ecological or physiological balance somewhere to allow conditions for cancer. And we might have had a cure for cancer long ago if humankind had been obedient to God and His revelation within His creation.

Then why doesn't God stop it? If He really loved, would He not do away with all the manifestations of evil and its consequences? Wouldn't He write the cure for cancer across the sky?

But whose freedom would He trample on if He did so? Whose freedom would you want God to remove? Mine? Yours? I suppose from another's standpoint, it would be all right if my freedom to choose were removed. But I do not want your freedom or mine removed. In that freedom is our opportunity to be and become; to laugh, to feel, to cry, to love. If that were removed, we would be only robots, chips in some computer somewhere. We would no longer be human beings.

It is a freedom which is real, deep, trusting, and powerful, as already indicated. We even have the freedom to determine how we react to our hurts, diseases, tragedies, and dying. Freedom would not be real to humanity if freedom to relate to the consequences of our choices and the choices of others was not present. As for me, I choose freedom over becoming a chip in a giant computer.

Natural Evil

It seems, however, that some evil in this world has nothing to do with moral evil. Consider earthquakes—what moral evil of human beings would bring an earthquake upon us?

First, we need to remember that nature is extremely benevolent, and it gives us joy. As George Buttrick wrote, "A Library of gratitude could be written on the fidelities of nature."[8]

And what a beautiful world. It "fits" us in so many ways. The rain, the wind, the sun, the trees, the rocks, and the colorful autumn leaves all have their place. As you look around and really see the beauty and beneficence of this world, you can know, as Buttrick claimed, the experience of Edna St. Vincent Millay's "fear." The world was so beautiful to Millay that she practically begged the Lord not to add another falling leaf or another bird's call to what she saw. The scene already was almost too beautiful for her soul to take.[9]

There are still earthquakes, hailstorms, and tornadoes. Only recently the news came that tornadoes ripped through parts of a neighboring state, killing several people and destroying some dreams as well. Such events seem to have no relationship to the choices or freedom of humanity. They seem to lie outside the moral sphere of existence. One might conclude, then, that such events are God's doing.

Are these events reserved by God so that He may terrorize us, or so that he may engage in mass punishment at whatever intervals He desires? Some have concluded that earthquakes, volcanoes, tornadoes, hurricanes, and other natural calamities are God's means of mass punishment. However, this view is in error.

God created an orderly world, a dependable world. Such order and dependability are evidences of God's love for us. As Elton Trueblood maintained, it is necessary for life to have a stable environment so life can develop. The pressures which build up in the heated interior of the earth and cause the earth's crust to be broken and lava to flow are law-abiding pressures. They operate according to the laws which make life predictable and tolerable for human existence. However, if people choose to live by a volcano, or choose not to heed its warnings, then they are hurt.[10]

Why doesn't God stop the volcano from erupting? Try to imagine a world in which God would suspend His laws whenever human beings refused to live responsibly. C. S. Lewis had a perceptive statement on this matter:

> We can, perhaps, conceive of a world in which God corrected the results of this abuse of free will by His creatures at every moment: so that a wooden beam became soft as grass when it was used as a weapon, and the air refused to obey me if I attempted to set up in it the sound waves that carry lies or insults. But such a world would be one in which wrong actions were impossible, and in which, therefore, freedom of the will would be void.[11]

We have disrupted the harmony between humanity and God and between humanity and creation so that we experience the things that hurt us, even "natural evils." Therefore, the blame for evil and its consequences are placed at the feet of humanity, not at the throne of God.

While we cannot be certain where a tornado will hit, human beings could be concerned enough about others to build structures that can withstand tornadoes. We do not exactly put human beings first in our activity in this world. The profit motive usually is more important. The cars we build, for example, are not built for the ultimate good of people. They offer very little protection to passengers inside when an accident occurs. If the good of human beings had been the corporate goal of all human activity from the beginning, would we build unsafe cars? Would cancer ever have happened? Would we have built cities next to volcanoes? Would our structures be earthquake proof? Admittedly, the question cannot be answered since, from the beginning, the welfare of humanity has not been the corporate goal of human activity.

If we think that we cannot live in harmony with a created order where volcanoes, tornadoes, and hurricanes exist, perhaps this is evidence of how far we have fallen in sin from the harmony which God intended for people to have. It certainly is evidence of how we have failed to grow and have dominion over the creation as God intended for us to have. It also may indicate how difficult it is for us to see what is in harmony with God's creation and what is not, to see and know what is true and what is not.

Consequently, laying the blame for evil at the feet of humanity does take seriously the matter of sin. We hurt not only ourselves but others when we sin. We disrupt the harmony of their existence and ours. We also contribute disharmony to the context of our existence which adds to the burden of those who come after us. The sins of the fathers do follow the children. Thus, recognizing that we might contribute to evil and its consequences, we are called to responsible living and responsible choosing. We can't blame the tempter, because he only tempts; he cannot choose for us. We are called to personal accountability.

Also, our discussion of God's love in relationship to evil has shown that God is not in any sense the perpetrator of evil. Rather, God's activity is to redeem us from evil. His love is our hope. The love does much more abound than the evil. We really can accept that God is for us (Rom. 8:30). The way of God with us is the way of love. God does not do evil. Human beings are responsible for evil.

Notes

1. Leonard Hodgson, *For Faith and Freedom* (London: SCM Press, LTD, 1968), p. 198.

2. C. S. Lewis, *The Problem of Pain* (New York: Macmillan Publishing Co., Inc., 1961), p. 92.

3. John K. Roth, "A Theodicy of Protest," *Encountering Evil*, ed. Stephan Davis (Atlanta: John Knox Press, 1981), p. 11.

4. John H. Hick, "An Irenaean Theodicy," *Encountering Evil*, ed. Stephan Davis (Atlanta: John Knox Press, 1981), pp. 41-42.

5. Ibid., p. 48

6. Ibid., p. 43

7. Stephen T. Davis, "Free Will and Evil," *Encountering Evil*, ed. Stephan Davis (Atlanta: John Knox Press, 1981), p. 74.

8. George A. Buttrick, *God, Pain, and Evil* (Nashville: Abingdon Press, 1966), p. 40.

9. Ibid, p. 41.

10. See David Elton Trueblood, *Philosophy of Religion* (New York: Harper & Row Publishers, 1957), pp. 253-254.

11. Lewis, *The Problem of Pain*, (New York: Macmillan Publishing Co., Inc., 1961), p. 33.

6

Love and Suffering

It is infinitely easier to suffer in obedience to a human command than in the freedom of one's own responsibility. It is infinitely easier to suffer with others than to suffer alone. It is infinitely easier to suffer publicly and honourably than apart and ignominiously. It is infinitely easier to suffer through staking one's life than to suffer spiritually. Christ suffered as a free man alone, apart and in ignominy, in body and spirit; and since then many Christians have suffered with him. (Dietrich Bonhoeffer).[1]

I don't know . . . sometimes I think I am an atheist. I've seen so many terrible things (A friend).

God shows his love . . . in that . . . Christ died for us (Rom. 5:8).

Rabbi Kushner became a nationally known figure almost overnight because of his book, *When Bad Things Happen to Good People.* The book was not intended to be psychological study nor a theological treatment although Kushner shares insights from both disciplines. Yet the book stayed on national best-seller lists for weeks. Why? Kushner touched a national nerve. People have perplexing, frustrating, and sometimes angry questions to ask God about suffering. Kushner courageously offered some answers to those questions from his personal pilgrimage of suffering and questioning. People were helped by his book.

However, in considering the relationship between God and

suffering, Kushner opted for a view of God that is disturbing—God is all-good but not all-powerful.[2]

The Problem of Suffering

Kushner's view of God illustrates the conflict that people have in relating their belief in God to the fact that people suffer. Suffering does seem to speak heavily against the existence of an all-powerful, loving God. First, some people reason, if God is all-powerful, then He cannot be totally good, because he does not use His power to stop evil and suffering. Second, if God is totally good, then He cannot be all-powerful, because He is unable to act out of His goodness to stop evil and suffering. How can an all-powerful God who loves permit suffering? Or, how can a loving God who is all-powerful allow suffering? How can we say that the way of God with us is the way of love when so much suffering and evil are present in life?

Few things work against belief in God in people's minds as do the suffering and pain which are everywhere in this world. It is the fundamental human problem. All cultures, both East and West, struggle to explain suffering and its relationship to a good Deity, or at least in relationship to what is good for people. The reason the presence of suffering poses such a problem for belief in God may be seen in this argument:

1) If God is all-powerful, He can prevent suffering;
2) If God is all-good, He will prevent suffering;
3) Suffering exists;
4) So there is no God.

If we could keep suffering at a distance, then the problem would not exist. But all of us suffer, and we do identify with and suffer with both loved ones and friends who suffer. The grandson sits across from me. He is frustrated and upset, and he has a right to be. His grandfather is experiencing great pain as he barely hangs onto life. Why, the grandson asks? Why does he have to suffer like this? He can understand why some bad people would suffer. But his grandfather served people all his life, cared for them, ministered to them. He lived by the standards of righteousness. He had been the stabilizer in the sea of storms. Now he suffers terribly. It just isn't fair. And he is right; it is not fair.

Read *A Grief Observed* by C. S. Lewis. This great Christian apologist, who could call to his service such lucid reasoning in defense of the faith in other contexts, withered under the grief caused by the suffering and death of his wife. Read the words which came out of his agony:

> Meanwhile, where is God? This is one of the most disquieting symptoms. When you are happy, so happy that you have no sense of needing Him, so happy that you are tempted to feel His claims upon you as an interruption, if you remember yourself and turn to Him with gratitude and praise, you will be—or so it feels— welcomed with open arms. But go to Him when your need is desperate, when all other help is vain, and what do you find? A door slammed in your face, and a sound of bolting and double bolting on the inside. After that, silence. You may as well turn away. The longer you wait, the more emphatic the silence will become. There are no lights in the windows. It might be an empty house. Was it ever inhabited? It seemed so once. And that seeming was as strong as this. What can this mean? Why is He so present a commander in our time of prosperity and so very absent a help in time of trouble?[3]

Such cases could be multiplied endlessly. We run into the questions. Why? Where is God at a time like this? Why would God do this? Why does He treat us so? We all know the questions elicited by suffering, but how are we to respond?

Some Negative Responses to Suffering

Of course the problem of suffering is not new, so consequently, human beings have devised many responses to it. I believe some responses are negative and unhelpful.

The major religions attempt answers. Buddha believed that suffering and existence are one. Part of his enlightenment included the four great truths about suffering: (1) the truth of suffering; (2) the cause of suffering; (3) the cessation of suffering; and (4) the way that leads to the cessation of suffering.

According to the law of Karma which Buddha proposed, a person is born back into life again and again to work out the results of past deeds. A person's deeds create an overplus of reward and punishment, and one must live again until the reward and punishment are exhausted. However, if in living again, you add other deeds, then the cycle will continue as long as there are deeds to be rewarded or punished, which means that you will continue to suffer.

Deeds spring from desire, Buddha taught. Desire must be done away with. The goal is to get to a passionless, actionless state—a state of existence known as Nirvana. In a sense, Nirvana means that the personality ceases to exist. To me, such existence is not existence as we really are. God created us the way we are intentionally. The effort to deny existence in itself is a passion or desire. Buttrick said,

> But common sense, the response of average men to the beckonings of nature and history, will reply that the death of desire is the death of the person: the operation is successful, but the patient dies. As for me, the image of the Buddha spells not peace, but complacent dessication.[4]

The Hindu belief is that we suffer in this life because of sins in a previous life. Your state of reincarnation, whether a bat or a human being, for instance, depends upon how good or how bad you were in the previous life. However, it seems grossly unfair for a baby to begin with a soul burdened and darkened by a previous life. In addition, if it were true that we are reincarnated, we do not remember the past sins.[5] I don't accept reincarnation and neither do I believe we suffer from sins in a previous life.

The view of Islam is that the good and evil which we experience are both the will of God. God has determined all that will happen to us. What humanity must do is submit to His will.[6]

However, some suffering that happens simply cannot be attributed to a good and loving God. If so, God would deny the reality of His goodness which He revealed in His Son. This is another view which leaves us cold and seeking the warmth of answers from some other source. If God is love, and God's way with us is love, He will not do evil to us and cause us suffering.

Some try to deny the existence of suffering. The Christian Science approach is to look upon pain as an error in the human mind. Most of us do not believe that. Pain is real. It is not simply an error of the mind. Of course, many of us have known of cases of psychosomatic suffering. Even imagined pain, however, hurts; and the fact that we can imagine pain indicates our human limitation about which we may ask, "Why do we suffer because of this limitation?" When we can touch the open wound, when grief rushes upon us by a sudden chain of unanticipated events, we are forced to admit the reality of pain and suffering.

Some have said that suffering is good for us. It builds character. It causes us to be sensitive to the suffering of others. While using suffering to build one's character or to make one more sensitive to the suffering of others is a healthy thing to do, this does not mean that suffering itself is good. Witness the fact that some people have become bitter and mean out of their suffering. Some with guilty consciences even have desired suffering in order to emotionally whip themselves for past mistakes and failures. Such people will make themselves suffer if it doesn't come to them naturally, which also reveals an unhealthy emotional state. At the same time, there is some suffering so devastating that a person is robbed of an ability to respond at all. At that point a person is dependent upon others.

George Buttrick rightly reminded us that suffering is incipient death: "The doctor asks, 'Where is the pain?' He looks for the place where incipient death has breached the wall."7 There is nothing inherently good in suffering.

Of course suffering may at times indicate that good is being done. The athlete training himself for the race or the student struggling to pass a test may push his mind and body until a certain amount of pain is there. Or, a person may take a moral stand on a certain issue and find herself rejected or overtly persecuted for her belief and action. However, suffering is not sought in any case, but a good is sought, and we would rather have the good without the suffering.

Another response to suffering is simply to run from its reality. A mother did this when her son died suddenly from an undiagnosed cause. She built a shell around herself and tried to construct a world in which her son was still alive. She tried to escape the pain caused by her son's death by closing out the real world. You perhaps can imagine the psychological devastation this suppression of the truth did to her. What perhaps one might not think to imagine is the harm done to her husband and the other children of the family. The grief, pain, and suffering were multiplied many times as a result of her refusal to deal with reality. It is absolutely necessary to accept the reality of suffering and to deal with it in healthy ways when it comes. Only then can it be kept from the status of a demon raging in us and raging upon those around us.

Of course, one can even accept suffering in the wrong way. I have heard people say, unfortunately, that suffering of some kind is a cross that God has laid upon them to bear. Why blame suffering on God?

Jesus told His disciples that following Him meant taking up one's cross (Matt. 16:24). How does one take up a cross? There is only one thing that happened on a cross in New Testament times—someone died. It was the electric chair of that time. It was a place of execution. So Jesus said in effect, "Take up your death and follow me." One is to die to self-centeredness, to selfishness, and live for Christ. Suffering may come as people take up their crosses and follow Christ, but the suffering comes as the way of Christ runs counter to the way of evil, not from overcoming self-centeredness.

If we believe that our suffering is laid upon us by God, then we cannot handle it as we should. To say in a spirit of resignation, "Well, this suffering is just the cross that God has given me to bear," is to say that you had nothing to say in the matter.

While we must bear our own pain and share the burden of others, a cowardly resignation to its reality is an inadequate response. Jesus bore a cross. He did so, however, aggressively. He used it. He conquered it. He turned it into redemption, about which I will say more later. Suffering is not to rule *us*, we are to rule *it*, turn it to purpose in some way. Such response requires courage.

However, you can accept suffering in bitterness, and become bitter at the whole world. Bitterness in this case is different from anger. It has been established that expressing anger is one of the stages of grief caused by suffering. Anger can be a rather normal and anticipated reaction to suffering, especially intense suffering. However, to stay in the anger stage would be improper to the well-being of the sufferer and those around him.

Others write suffering off as a matter of getting what is deserved. An element of truth is in this claim. Some of our sins cause bad consequences immediately. But in many cases such a claim is not applicable. In the Old Testament Book of Job, Job's friends proposed that his suffering resulted from unrighteousness on his part. Job rejected that explanation, realizing that he had done nothing to earn the kind of suffering that came to him. We do not have to search long for examples of undeserved suffering. Consider Jesus, who suffered exceedingly and did not deserve it. Consider the child born with a crippled limb because of a physician's mistake in the delivery. Much evidence exists that much pain comes to the innocent, and it is undeserved.

One of the dangers of the "you get what you deserve" approach is that it can be taken to ridiculous conclusions. In one of our student pastorates, my wife and three-year-old son missed prayer service one Wednesday night because our son had a greater need than my wife's attendance at church. A church member asked about her absence, and my wife gave the logical explanation. The church member responded by warning my wife that she had better be careful of using our son as an excuse. She had known of cases where God simply removed such excuses!

What a regrettable view of God who loves our son more than is humanly possible. We must be careful how we interpret and apply the "getting what we deserve" explanation of suffering. One mother with young children, for example, was distressed because she was afraid that God would cause her children to suffer for reasons that she could not name other than she believed that God caused all suffering, assigning suffering arbitrarily or for hidden reasons which no human being could know. While she loved God, she also had this fear about God. She needed to know that the way of God with us is the way of love.

Then how can we speak of suffering and a God who loves in the same context? The answer is much the same as that answer we gave to the existence of evil in chapter 2. We must set suffering in the context of the disharmony caused by humanity's errant ways. The innocent suffer, and even the guilty suffer too much, because we are born into a context of imperfection caused by humanity's wrongdoing. God does not cause the suffering; human beings invite it in, create it. God in His love works against suffering. He works to restore order and harmony.

Remember, God must work so as not to remove human freedom. We could attempt to fault God by claiming that He should have taken over and wiped out evil with its attendant suffering inflicted upon the innocent as well as the guilty. But God did not make us guilty. We did that. God did not make suffering. We ourselves rip holes in human existence by our sins and allow it in.

But what about those who are in circumstances which prevent freedom of choice? A totalitarian ruler, for example, may disorient and destroy another's life by imprisonment and torture. The mind can be manipulated and even destroyed by drugs. A person suffers because of freedom taken away. Unfortunately, people do use their freedom to take away the freedom of others. Human beings have the tendency to pervert and abuse their freedom, and the innocent suffer. This opens up another, although related, investigation. But for the purposes of our thesis, God does not do anything to abuse the privilege of freedom He gives to us. Part of that freedom is to act and live responsibly toward others so that others may have the opportunity to live and act responsibly. The freedom to be entails heavy responsibility as well as great joy, but people abuse the privilege and hurt others.

"Then God should have made us where we could not sin like that," the objector might argue. But God did make us that way. We have a choice; we can choose righteousness and fellowship with Him. "But God should have made us where that was the only choice we could make." Ah, but there goes freedom, and we are back once again to the puppet or computer-chip status. And who wants that? The puppet doesn't live, although it may appear to do so as its limbs and features are made to move. A computer chip does not live, although on it may be stored information and actions that seem almost human. I'll take the risk of living with the freedom to choose any day above being like a puppet or a computer chip.

Some Positive Responses to Suffering

Part of our freedom to choose means that we must react responsibly to suffering. How are we to handle the reality? The beginning point is to realize that we cannot deal with collective and individual suffering in our own strength alone. We need each other; we need the relationship with one another by which we share one another's burdens, including suffering. The church, the people of God, should provide that relationship for suffering humanity. Its invitation and action must be that of Jesus, whose body the church is: "Come to me, all who labor and are heavy laden, and I will give you rest" (Matt. 11:28).

Most of all, however, we need the sustaining relationship with God, whose way with us is the way of love. How we think about God determines how we respond to the relationship He offers us. Thinking that God is the instigator of our suffering makes it more difficult to enter into the close relationship which He extends to us. God does not desire that we suffer, nor did He ever intend it. We need to understand, once for all, that God is *for* us—that His way with us is the way of love.

Another positive response we can make is to accept the reality of suffering—not that we approve it or that we will tolerate it if something can be done about it. The Bible does not deal very much with the origin of suffering, but it does deal with its reality. Consider the man who was blind since his birth (John 9:1-7). The disciples asked why, but Jesus did not answer as to the cause. The effect was there, and He was ready to deal with it. If we are to respond to suffering appropriately, then we must not hide from it, run from its reality, or be bitter about it. So, we accept its reality, determined to deal with our suffering in healthy ways.

Assuming, of course, that we will use all the political, economic, and medical ways available to us to eliminate suffering, how are we to deal with it in a healthy way, practically and theologically? As indicated already, the writers of both the Old and New Testaments were not especially concerned about the origin of suffering. Rather, they were more interested in the purpose and reason for suffering. The Old Testament shows various understandings and responses to suffering.

Various writers understood suffering as divine punishment, or divine wrath (Pss. 38:3; 42:5,9). Job did not understand the reason or purpose in his suffering, so he just chalked it up to the wisdom of God, a wisdom which was incomprehensible to him (Job 42:2-3). Others in the Old Testament viewed suffering as educational, a divine teaching tool by which people could be led back to the way of God (Ps. 20:6; 2 Chron. 20:9-10).

The Old Testament also raises the question as to why its prophets, and messengers of God, should suffer—sometimes much more than others (Jer. 8:18-21; 15:15; Ps. 44:23). The conclusion was that you can suffer vicariously for someone else. Consider the Suffering Servant passages in Isaiah: "In solidarity with his people, the Servant of God has taken vicariously upon himself the punishment of his nation" (Isa. 53:2-12).[8] Thus, the germ of the idea that suffering can be a redemptive activity was expressed at this point.

The views of the Old Testament are found in the New Testament, but they are viewed in a different light—the light of the suffering, death, and resurrection of Jesus Christ. He suffered as the sinless One who took on Himself the suffering of the whole world, giving Himself in behalf of all (Rom. 3:25; 5:6-8; 1 Pet. 2:24). In other words, He entered into the deepest suffering of humankind in order to redeem every person to life and freedom.

Jesus turned suffering into redemption. He did not debate the origin of suffering. He seemed to ask, "What can this suffering serve?" The cross is the ultimate testimony of how Jesus turned suffering into redemption.

The followers of Jesus did the same thing. They put redemptive character into suffering. Paul said, for example, that by his suffering he completed "what is lacking in Christ's afflictions for the sake of his body" (Col. 1:24). In other words, Paul's suffering was being turned to use by Paul himself to help build the church. First Peter 4:12-13 has much the same thrust. It isn't that Paul and other early Christians were seeking suffering. Rather, they were encouraged to turn their suffering into good in some way.

Consider that the sufferer can turn his suffering into a force to aid others. Courage, for example, can be communicated. As one sees another courageously turning his suffering into a positive force in some way, his own courage grows. Recently I visited an elderly lady who has suffered much. She is tough. She lies on her bed and plans her course of action, and her options are not many. When others come into the room, she communicates interest in and concern for them. There is a flow of ministry going out from her. People come to minister to her and find themselves ministered to and encouraged. I encountered the doctor outside her room, and he asked, "Have you ever seen a person of such attitude and courage?" She was turning her suffering into redemption.

So, when suffering comes, we have a choice to make. We can turn our suffering into continuous complaint, into self-pity, into bitterness, or into redemption in some way.

Paul Tournier tells of the Oxford Group Movement, which had meant so much to his life, which was born out of a courageous act by Frank Buchman. Buchman was director of an institute, and he had a serious disagreement with the committee assigned to work with the institute. He was dismissed from his position. Later, he retreated to a little chapel, filled with anger and bitterness. While in the chapel, he felt the call of God to admit his own faults, to forgive the members of the committee, and to ask them to forgive him. He wrote a letter to each committee member, confessing his faults and asking for forgiveness.

The courage of his act became known and spread like wildfire among the students. People found the courage to put their own lives in order. The movement spread beyond Oxford to other countries, where Tournier came under the influence of that same kind of courageous admission and action. All this happened because one person decided to act redemptively in response to his own suffering.[9]

As we talked about redemptive suffering in a seminar, one

student told of the action and attitudes of his mother in her suffering. She died of cancer while he was young. The story he told of her prior to her death was a story of concern for and ministry to her family. She prepared them for the event. She demonstrated courageous faith. Her example built courage into the whole situation and character into her family. She turned her suffering into redemptive action.

Suffering, A Community Event

We must remember that most suffering occurs in one way or another in the context of community—a community of family and/or friends. Whenever a person responds to suffering with courage, others may be encouraged. Courage spreads; character is built; community is built. At the same time, the community can gather around the person suffering and have the courage to enter into the situation of the sufferer. Then the sufferer draws upon the supportive courage of others. In this way, the sufferer and the community turn suffering into redemption. The church, of course, should be the community of faith that enters into the situation of the sufferer. God through His people can turn suffering into redemption.

Suzanne Fouché, a friend of Paul Tournier's, intended to study medicine for her life's work. However, she was struck in adolescence by a bone disease. The disease caused her to be confined in one hospital after another for eighteen years. She despaired; she even rebelled. The disease imposed painful problems and difficult struggles.

When still young, she noticed what confinement did to patient morale. From her bed she reached out to other patients with the simple message, "Do what you can!" She organized them into small groups doing all kinds of activities. The movement spread into a charity which set up homes for rehabilitation of the physically handicapped. Thousands of lives were transformed as a result of her attitude and work. Tournier characterized her life as one in which she said a bigger yes to God than she did to her suffering. She turned her suffering redemptively toward the community around her, and the community, in turn, acted redemptively.[10]

This is the choice we have in the midst of our suffering and the suffering around us. We can choose to say a bigger yes to God than to our suffering. We can do so as we remember that God places the resurrection event alongside every event of suffering. We can trust Him, and accept the reality of suffering, and turn it into redemption.

Ultimately, the individual and the community reach their limits in making suffering redemptive. Suffering, as stated earlier, is really incipient death. Eventually death comes to all of us. What then can a human being do? Nothing, really, except to turn toward God. And God is ready. Right alongside death and all death-threatening situations, God places the resurrection event.[11] Jesus endured terrible suffering, even to the point of death. He placed the whole matter into God's hands, aggressively taking on suffering and death in the light of faith in His Father. Did the Father disappoint Him? Did He let Him down? No, God raised Him up. It is the nature of God to raise up life out of suffering and death. Suffering, incipient death, does not and will not win. We will not lose life. We are called, therefore, to act redemptively in our suffering and to trust in God.

In summary, then, suffering does not speak against the existence of a good and loving all-powerful God. God is on our side. He is *for* us, not against us; His way with us is the way of love. We are called to act redemptively in the midst of our suffering. This is noeasy task. We can do so by saying a bigger yes to God than we do to our suffering. In addition, God lays alongside every suffering eventthe resurrection event, which is the ultimate and definitive answer to suffering. God is the One who overcomes suffering, which is incipient death, and death itself. God is the Giver of life, not theTaker. It is so because the way of God with us is the way of love.

Notes

1. Dietrich Bonhoeffer, *Letters and Papers from Prison,* rev. and ed. by Eberhard Bethge (New York: The Macmillan Company, 1953), pp. 14-15.

2. Harold S. Kushner, *When Bad Things Happen to Good People* (New York: Avon, 1983), pp. 42-45.

3. C. S. Lewis, *A Grief Observed* (New York: The Seabury Press, 1961), p. 9.

4. George Arthur Buttrick, *God, Pain, and Evil* (New York: Abingdon Press, 1966), pp. 27-28.

5. Ibid., pp. 29-30

6. E. Stanley Jones, *Christ and Human Suffering* (New York: Abingdon Press, 1961), p. 60.

7. Buttrick, *God, Pain, and Evil,* p. 26

8. O. A. Piper, "Suffering," *The Interpreter's Dictionary of the Bible,* IV, ed. by George A. Buttrick (New York: Abingdon Press, 1962), p. 452.

9. Paul Tournier, *Creative Suffering* (San Francisco: Harper & Row, 1981) p. 99.

10. Ibid., pp. 91-92

11. Buttrick, in *God, Pain, and Evil,* found this to be God's definitive answer to the question of suffering.

7

Love and Judgment: Judgment Not of God

He gave man the power to thwart His will, that, by means of that same power, he might come at last to do His will in a higher kind and way than would otherwise have been possible to him. (George MacDonald).[1]

Is the God of the Old Testament different from the God of the New Testament? (A teacher's question to the class).

God shows his love for us (Rom. 5:8).

William Barclay, the Scottish New Testament scholar, sometimes took controversial positions on interpretations of the Scriptures. Once, when he was interviewed following a series of talks for the British Broadcasting Company, he related the experience of knowing God's sustaining strength during and after the time his twenty-one-year-old daughter drowned in a yachting accident. A listener in Northern Ireland, angry over something Barclay had said in his radio Bible study, wrote an anonymous letter. The letter stated, "Dear Dr. Barclay, I know now why God killed your daughter; it was to save her from being corrupted by your heresies."[2]

But Barclay knew that God did not go around drowning people's daughters in order to punish them. Had he known the writer's address, he said that he would have written back, in pity not in anger, in words which John Wesley said to someone: "Your God is my devil."[3]

Unfortunately, some people do view all bad events and experiences as the direct visitation of divine punishment. Not all judgment is judgment of a bad kind, for judgment can be good. Judgment can be used to examine and evaluate the good and determine where approval should be expressed or reward should be given. Judgment can also be good when it involves positive discipline. A parent can say to a child, for example, "I believe that you are headed in a direction which is not good for you. Because I love you, I demand that you take the following steps to correct yourself." The steps, while tough and demanding, would not be harmful physically nor emotionally but positive in their intent. All of God's judgment is positive and involves constructive discipline. His judgment arises out of love. In love is the only way in which God's judgment can come to us because His very nature is love, and He cannot and will not act contrary to His nature.

Because of an inadequate understanding of judgment, God is sometimes viewed as existing and sovereign, but as a mean, temperamental Sovereign who will destroy someone loved as a means of punishing someone else. I have even heard the statement, said by a grandparent of a grandchild who died, "We loved him too much, so God took him." I realize that such a statement can be said with a terrible seriousness and innocence, but it is wrong. It is contrary to God's revelation of Himself in Christ, His Son. We need to clear up some confusion at this point. We can do so by first distinguishing as best we can the judgment which is not of God.

The Wrath of God?

It is possible to misunderstand wrath and its place in God's judgment. All judgment in one sense is God's judgment. God permits certain judgments, for such permission is tied up with the freedom which He grants to us to choose and to be. The "wrath of God," however, still worries people. What happens, some people wonder, when God's toughness turns into anger? A teenage boy is driving home late at night when a car coming

from the opposite direction wanders across the middle line and
hits him in a head-on crash. What could the boy or someone else
have done to cause God to get that angry? Is this a wrathful
action of God since "the wrath of God is revealed from heaven
against all ungodliness and wickedness of men" (Rom. 1:18)?
Whenever something goes wrong, is God venting His wrath to
one degree or another in order to shake us up a bit? Should we
then fear the ultimate "shake-up" when we may be maimed or
killed because God is very angry at us or someone else?

I must confess that if God were one who visited wrath upon
us, judged us, by killing those whom we love, then I could not
think of Him in any positive terms. In fact, such a God would
become as Wesley indicated, "my devil." A good human being,
even finite and limited as a good human being may be, does not
kill the loved ones of a person in order to right a wrong. And
God is so much greater in goodness than a good person that
there is really no comparison. Are we then to ascribe to God a
level of action and being lower than that of a good person?
"But," someone argues, "we cannot compare God and a good
person, because God is God and He can do what He wants to
do." Agreed. But "God is love," and what He wants to do is
never destructive. What He does is always good, just, holy, and
loving.

It is possible to come away from a reading of the Old and New
Testaments with the image of an angry, wrathful God who is out
to get revenge against humanity for its sins. But that depends
on how we interpret as we read.

God does not create destructive judgment. He simply allows
people the judgment they have made for themselves. What do
we do then with Old Testament passages of Scripture that seem
to present God as destructive, accounts that seem to say that
God orders the killing of innocent babies and children, even the
unborn in a mother's womb? And how do we interpret a situation in which God is said to use evil as an agency? Does God,
whose way with us is the way of love, kill babies, children, and

the unborn? Does God, who has no evil and no darkness in Him, use evil as an instrument? There are different approaches to be taken in dealing with these questions.

In some cases, Old Testament writers and prophets did not bother to distinguish between what God did as an action of love and what God allowed to happen as the result of human choosing and action. The Hebrew mind at times attributed everything to God without bothering to distinguish between permitted judgment and the active judgment of God.

However, permitted judgment raises another question. If God allows destruction when He could stop it, doesn't that mean that in reality God does the judgment? Since God's way with us is the way of *agapē* (love), I would have to answer negatively to the question. Again, God allows us freedom and the results of our choices which we make out of that freedom. We reap what we sow. To say that God sends a nation upon Israel to destroy Israel means to me that God allowed Israel to reap the results of her own choices. They turned from God and got themselves, for example, into political and economic trouble. The freedom is real. The choice is real, and what happens to people ultimately is determined by the individual and especially the collective choices of humanity.

The prophet Amos understood the importance of that freedom and that choosing. He said to Israel, "Seek good, and not evil, that you may live" (Amos 5:14).

Amos knew that Israel had chosen wrongly and had set themselves upon a destructive course. He tried to warn them of the destruction they had invited in upon themselves. Unfortunately, the innocent also suffer when there is such individual and collective sinfulness. Jesus Himself suffered and died to save us. He was the only truly innocent Person in all of humanity, yet see how He suffered.

The Bible is the inspired Word of God. In that Word, God reveals who He is. As we read the Bible, we read about what God revealed of Himself. God reveals Himself as Creator,

Deliverer, and Sustainer. He reveals Himself also as Savior. As Creator, Deliverer, Sustainer, and Savior, He acts out of who He is—"God is love."

The Bible, however, also reveals who human beings are and how they are. They are revealed just as they are, with all the limitations and blemishes showing. We see them, as we read and struggle to understand God, and how their sinfulness (and now ours) was a barrier to their understanding. Sometimes they failed to understand God. Sometimes the Israelites tried to make God into a warrior God and the property of Israel. Sometimes they tried to force God into their own religious mold. God, of course, cannot be owned or molded, for He is God.

The context of Scripture will help us to understand how to put some Old Testament passages in perspective with God's love. The ultimate way, however, is to look to Christ. Christ is the ultimate revelation of God Himself; Christ is *the* Word of God (John 1:1-14). So everything said or thought about God must be examined in the light of Jesus Christ. If I have an interpretation which is contrary to the nature of God as revealed inChrist, then I must reinterpret, because God is faithful, and He does not contradict Himself.

We acknowledge that God is the all-powerful, all-knowing Sovereign who can do as He pleases. But how does He please to do? He acts out of His nature, which is *agapē*. Jesus came to seek and save the lost, not destroy them. He reached out to the despised and rejected. He warned the religionists in no uncertain terms of the destruction they were making for themselves. He died for them and us. He loved them and He loves us. That is the way the sovereign God pleases to do. If He did not, but chose to turn His power to angry destruction in order to root out every bit of evil, who among us could stand? He chooses to act out of love and to redeem us from our evil.

Consider now a New Testament statement on wrath. Paul wrote in Romans 1:18, "For the wrath of God is revealed from heaven against all ungodliness and wickedness of men." Now, doesn't that say it? God is eager, isn't He, for the opportunity to get even with us because of our wickedness? Doesn't "wrath" mean that God gets angry and loses His temper? The bad things that happen are the result of God's wrath—or so someone might reason. Some might even go so far as to reason that since bad things have happened (and they happen to everyone), God is against them and there isn't much point in believing Him and following His will. After all, "The wrath of God is revealed from heaven against all ungodliness."

But consider carefully what Paul meant by wrath. First there is the history of the word. *Wrath* is not used by Paul to refer to one venting one's passions upon another. Rather, Paul uses it more in terms of an objective reality;[3] that is to say, it is a kind of existence in which one chooses to live. It is a process, an effect, which one has chosen to embrace. It is "from heaven" because God allows a human being to choose such an existence.

According to C. H. Dodd, the prophets of the Old Testament moved the idea of the wrath of God out of the mysterious into the realm of cause and effect: "Sin is the cause, disaster is the effect."[4] Wrath is the effect of human sin. Human sin brings disaster. God saves from disaster by His mercy. Mercy is not the effect of human beings; mercy originates from God's side.[5] Paul used the term "wrath of God" then, "not to describe the attitude of God to man, but to describe an inevitable process of cause and effect in the moral universe."[6] In other words, wrath is humanity's doing which God permits because God has given humanity freedom to choose.

Consequences

All of us, then, live with the results of our sins, results which are bad because of their very nature. In addition, because we live in a world of people, we sometimes experience the results of the sins of others. The consequences of our sins and the sins of others upon ourselves constitute judgment, but they fall under a category of what we already have called permitted judgment.

In 2 Kings 24:1-4, we read that Jehoiakim rebelled against Nebuchadnezzar. As a result, the writer said that bands of Chaldeans, Syrians, Moabites, and Ammonites were sent against Judah at the direction of the Lord. However, verse 3 indicates that this judgment came because of the sins of Manasseh. The rule of Manasseh was characterized by idolatry and violence. "He did much evil in the sight of the Lord" (2 Kings 21:6). God permitted the consequences of their choices and actions. Judah made its own judgment and destruction.

To read that the Lord did such judgment and destruction, as indicated in 2 Kings 24:3, was characteristic of the Jewish way of thinking. As Sovereign, everything came under the dictates of God. They did not bother sometimes to differentiate between God's causing and God's allowing. It was not God's wish that destruction even come upon Israel, or anyone else, but His will to make people truly free means that He had to allow people the consequences of their choices. We know that God does not cause everything. He does not cause us to sin, for example. God does however permit things to happen, even the bad things.

Inherent in the consequences of sin is disaster—on the collective level and the individual level. God warns against evil; He works against the consequences of evil; and so often His grace and mercy win without our cooperation. But God ultimately does permit the consequences of our choices. He is involved in the consequences insofar as He permits us the right to our bad judgment and the negative consequences which that brings.

God's warning about the consequences of wrong choices and actions are so specific. The words ring out from Ezekiel, "The soul that sins shall die" (18:20), words with implications and applications beyond their immediate context. The warning echoes in the New Testament: "The wages of sin is death" (Rom. 6:23). In the great "unto the least of these" passage (Matt.

25:31-46), the judgment is the permitting of the consequences of choices and actions. Those who give food, water, friendship, clothing, and visit the prisoners act and choose out of the nature of Christ, and they receive the judgment of "inherit the kingdom prepared for you" (v. 34). The others receive the judgment of "Depart from me, you cursed, into the eternal fire" (v. 41), which is a permitting of the results of their choices and actions out of their character, a character lived apart from a relationship with God. God's permitting or allowing the consequences of our sins is His way of showing He is against sin.

On the other hand, people can choose to allow the consequences of God's action into their lives. Following Ezekiel 18:-20, the prophet emphasized that the wicked can choose to turn from their sins and live (vv. 21-22). Of course the second half of Romans 6:23 is that "the free gift of God is eternal life in Jesus Christ our Lord." The consequences of God's action into life which a person can choose are forgiveness, strength, help, purpose, deliverance, salvation, and others.

In Galatians 5:19-24, Paul told of the works of the flesh and the fruit of the Spirit. The works of the flesh are immorality, impurity, and a long list of other destructive experiences. Paul warned that those who do such things "shall not inherit the kingdom of God" (v. 21). The fruit of the Spirit is love, joy, peace, and a long list of other positive, constructive experiences of life. By "flesh" Paul meant not the flesh of one's body but a state of existence in which one lived. That state of existence, or life, was one over against God. "Spirit," on the other hand, means life lived in relationship to God. A person chooses to live in one existence or the other. The life of "flesh" beings destructive, bad experiences. The life of Spirit, life with God, brings positive life-developing and life-giving experiences. God offers the life giving, and wants everyone to have that experience, but He permits the others. The other brings its own destruction.

Sermons have been preached on hell in which the emphasis was that people go to eternal punishment because God sends them there. However, people are eternally separated from God because God allows the ultimate consequences of their choices. If we look at hell—the name for total and eternal separation from God—from a different perspective, who is it that makes hell a reality? Is it not humankind? If we choose to separate ourselves from the salvation of God, haven't we by choosing called into existence the negative judgment upon us and our own eternal separation from God? God can do no other than to grant a person the eternal death to which he has consigned himself. Everything that God has done from the very beginning and is doing now is against that kind of destiny for a person. God does not choose eternal death for us. He chooses life for us and makes it available to us as a free gift.

But He allows the other. That is how real this freedom to choose which He gives is. Frank Stagg wrote:

> It is not because God wills that any be lost but that he wills the freedom of salvation. God does not withdraw from the freedom he gives, even though we use it to self-destruct.

He then quoted G. B. Caird's comment on Revelation 20:10:

> The lake of fire stands at the end of the world's story as a proof of the dignity of man, whom God will never reduce to the status of puppet by robbing him of his freedom of choice.[7]

When we choose to be gods of our own lives, not allowing God to save and to reign, we do make our own destruction. Henri J. M. Nouwen told an ancient tale from India in which four sons were deciding what specialty they would master. They decided to search the earth, make their choices, and learn their special sciences. After deciding where they would meet again, they separated, searched, and mastered. When they met, the first indicated that he could make the flesh of a creature, even if he had only a piece of bone of the creature. The second said that he had mastered the science whereby he could create the hair and skin of the creature if it had flesh and bones. The third announced that he could create the limbs of the creature if it had the flesh, bone, and hair. The fourth claimed that he had the final stroke for the creative process, because he could give it life.

So they set off in search of a bone. Unfortunately, the piece of bone they found was that of a lion, and they did not know it. So they gave it flesh, skin, hair, limbs, and finally, life. The lion shook its heavy mane, roared, and sprang upon them with its vicious teeth and terrible claws. He killed his creators and vanished into the jungle.[8]

When we act as gods of our own life, we do create our own destruction. We need to respond to the love of God so that He may save us from ourselves. Otherwise, we bring negative judgment on ourselves, individually, and on humanity as a whole, and we are totally responsible for the consequence. God's consequences, however, are good for us, because His way with us always, even in judgment, is the way of love.

Notes

1. *George MacDonald, an Anthology,* ed. by C. S. Lewis (New York: Macmillan Publishing Co., Inc., 1978), p. 101.

2. William Barclay, *A Spiritual Autobiography* (Grand Rapids: William B. Eerdmans Publishing Company, 1977), p. 52.

3. Ibid.

4. C. H. Dodd, *The Epistle of Paul to the Romans, The Moffatt New Testament Commentary,* ed. by James Moffatt (London: Hodder and Stoughton, 1932), p. 23.

5. Ibid.

6. Ibid.

7. Frank Stagg, "A Whole Man Made Well," in *The Struggle for Meaning,* ed. by W. P. Tuck (Valley Forge, Pa.: Judson Press, 1977), p. 73.

8. Henri J. M. Nouwen, *The Wounded Healer* (Garden City, N.Y.: Image Books, pp. 5-6.

8

Love and Judgment: Judgment of God

I am content, O Father, to leave my life in Thy hands, believing that the very hairs upon my head are numbered by Thee. I am content to give over my will to Thy control, believing that I can find in Thee a righteousness that I could never have won for myself. I am content to leave all my dear ones to Thy care, believing that Thy love for them is greater than my own. I am content to leave in Thy hands the causes of truth and of justice, and the coming of Thy Kingdom in the hearts of men, believing that my ardour for them is but a feeble shadow of Thy purpose. To Thee, O God, be glory forever. Amen. (A Prayer by John Baillie).[1]

I don't understand how judgment can be an expression of love. They seem opposite to me. (A student).

God shows his love for us (Rom. 5:8).

One of my earliest experiences concerning God was one of fear. By fear I do not mean a healthy reverence and respect, because I feared that God was out to get me. I suppose that my attitude was influenced to some degree by some of the preaching I heard. One preacher, I remember, yelled and repeatedly slapped the pulpit as he preached. He usually was angry about something, although I am not certain now, nor do I think I understood then, what angered him. I am sure he had reason, but I thought that he represented the voice of God and that God must be angry at me. I suppose I felt as one man said he felt as a child when he sometimes lay awake at night, terrified at what punishments an almighty God had concocted for a little boy who had not been very good that day. My view of God was exactly opposite of His revelation in Jesus, the one to whom the children ran with delight. I wish my beginning experience had been different. Thanks to the gracious, tough love of God revealed in Jesus Christ, I have overcome that unhealthy fear.

But some people haven't. They still retain images and emotions about God from a frightened childhood. Perhaps parents used a distorted picture of God in order to discipline them. One of the most damaging things a parent can say to a child is, "If you act like that, God is not going to love you." Or, "God doesn't love little girls who do that." Or, "God doesn't like you if you are bad."

Of course God loves and likes the bad person. One of the reasons we come to God is to be liberated from the badness which we feel and to be delivered from future badness. Out of His love, God acts graciously to forgive and restore us again and again.

Basic Judgment

God has a foundational judgment which He made from the very beginning about his creative act of bringing humanity into existence. The opening chapter of Genesis tells us no less than seven times that God's creative work was good (Gen. 1:4,10,12,-18,21,25,31). So, human beings, the human race, are products of God's creative good work and, consequently, they are of inherent value and dignity. This is true for every person.

God likes us as human beings. He doesn't want us to be anything else. He certainly doesn't want us to be gods, nor does He wish us to be messiahs, for there is only one God and one Messiah. He made us as human beings, and He wants us to be human beings. God's basic judgment for us, then, is that we are individuals who are products of His creative good work. Someone might object that while that may have been true of Adam

and Eve, it is not true of us, because we are products of the
union of our fathers and mothers. But this does not make us any
less a creation of God, because parents only participate in the
creative work of God as a new life is brought into the world.
Parents do not make life, for God is the Giver of all life. At one
stage in his life my son had a poster hanging in his room which
said, "God likes me, He doesn't make junk." God's basic judgment is that He created good. Indeed, He would do no other,
because His nature is that of *agapē* love.

Some years ago, the book *I'm OK: You're OK* by Thomas A.
Harris became popular. Harris communicated basic psychological concepts in understandable form. The title tells the thrust
of the book—that we need to come to the view, if we are to have
wholeness, that I'm OK and the other person is OK, too. It is
inadequate to believe that I'm not OK and you're OK, or that
I'm OK and you're not, or that neither of us is OK. We need to
come to the point of knowing and feeling that we are both OK.[2]

That is the beginning point of God's judgment—I am OK, and
My fellow human being is OK. But that is not the stopping
point. For many reasons many people do not feel OK about
themselves, the reasons together adding up to what the Bible
accurately calls sin. A not-OK feeling alerts us to our need. We
have by our sins marred what God has created, including ourselves. How do we get the feeling again that we are OK? Ultimately, only God can do something about that, although we can
help in the process.

God's judgment is always to confront us in our state of not
being OK so that He may lead us to repent (turn around),
forgive us, and restore us. God's basic judgment, then, is that we
are the result of His creative love, that we are of value and
dignity, that we have marred the good which He created, and
that He judges in order to bring us to being OK again.

Discipline

God judges in a number of ways as He moves past the basic judgment. He judges the negative about us. The concept of God's judgment in the Bible carries with it the idea of God's punishment or discipline upon the unrighteous person and unrighteous acts.

It is widely accepted that parents who love their children with a healthy love will discipline their children for good. It is natural that, as people thought in terms of God's discipline, they would perceive it in terms of parent to child. The Proverbs offer a case in point:

My son, do not despise the Lord's discipline
 or be weary of his reproof,
for the Lord reproves him whom he loves,
 as a father the son in whom he delights (Prov. 3:11).

Of course, this is tough discipline out of a tough love, not some easygoing sentimentality that doesn't care about the person. Sentimentality allows us to be secure in our wrongdoing. Or the reverse may be true. Where there is no demand made upon us—no discipline—we may feel that we are somewhat worthless because no one cares whether we do right or wrong.

We should emphasize again, however, that God's discipline—His judgment—is never destructive. Just as a father or mother chooses a discipline that does not injure or destroy a child, because it is discipline out of a healthy love, so the loving Father, although His discipline is tough and demanding, does not mete out discipline that injures or destroys.

Then, what forms does the discipline take? How can we know that God's judgment and discipline are coming to us? In the previous chapter, some judgments were discussed which were not of God. These are negative and destructive. God's judgments are positive and redemptive. It is important for us to be sensitive to God's judgment in our lives, although it may be painful, because then we can be sensitive and responsive to God's discipline so that God can work His redeeming work in us. God's punishment and discipline should be welcomed by us, because they are always saving in their effect. To resist God's discipline is to continue in our self-destructive way by which we create our own destructive judgment, as indicated in the previous chapter.

Confrontation with Truth

One of the recognizable ways God judges us is by confrontation with His truth. God is truth and He deals with us in truth. He will not allow us to live by a lie without confronting us in some way.

Lewis Smedes, in beautiful expression, wrote: "Love, then, will not give evil a decent spot in God's world: love will not let evil sneak into a great and good scheme. Evil cannot gain respectability in the presence of love."[3] Smedes indicated that it is no wonder then that love "does not rejoice at wrong, but rejoices in the right," (1 Cor. 13:6). God rejoices in the right because it is the right that is good for us. God confronts us with His truth to rid evil from the grand and good scheme He has for us. It is the undisciplined, those who live by illusions or lies, who suffer the most and who are not free. God disciplines us with His truth for our good.

The case of Paul again provides an example. Paul persecuted the church. If anyone deserved to be struck down Paul did, as he later admitted. He even sanctioned murder as he guided persecution against the followers of Christ.

However, while Paul was en route to Damascus, Christ confronted Him with His presence. Paul saw the truth. Jesus was really the Christ as His followers proclaimed. In that confrontation, all the wrong that Paul had done against the church was seen clearly. Paul understood how wrong he had been and how much wrong he had done. The truth confronted him, and he was shattered by his wrongdoing. Paul was disciplined by confrontation with the reality of the living Christ.

Consider King David who committed adultery with Bathsheba and then had her husband murdered. David thought he had covered his wrongdoing well. One day Nathan the prophet came to see David. He told David a story about a wealthy man who owned many sheep raiding the fold of his neighbor and taking the one sheep which the neighbor had and needed so desperately. David became incensed at the crude heartlessness of the wealthy shepherd, and he was ready to bring judgment down on the thief. But Nathan looked the king straight in the eye, pointed his condemning finger at David, and said, "You are the man" (2 Sam. 12:7). David knew then that his wrongdoing was not hidden from God or anyone else. His sin of murder and adultery, as he stood in the light of the truth about himself, fell heavily upon his soul, and he was forced into mourning. He was disciplined by the judgment of God's truth.

Of course, people can deny the truth, run from truth's reality, and continue in their wrongdoing. In that case, there is no positive response to the discipline of God. People do not allow God's discipline to become a corrective so that more hurt, pain, and destructiveness can be avoided. Thus, people choose a discipline which is of their own making, and it is a destructive discipline. Hate begets hate; hurt begets hurt; wrongdoing begets wrongdoing; sin begets spiritual death. Refusing to live under the discipline of God's truth brings it own increasingly destructive impact.

The Judgment of Demand

Knowing God's truth, we realize God's demands upon us. We must be and act in that truth. This demand can be another form of judgment upon us if we are not living by the truth. He demands that we live righteously and that we be honest and just. He demands that we live up to our highest potential as human beings. For example, whenever I read, "Love your ene-

mies" as a demand from Christ upon my life, I am immediately
called into judgment. Have I loved my enemies? Have I even
loved those who are not my enemies? Do I have hostility toward
anyone in the church? Have I torn down someone's character
rather than seeking to help build? Do I realize that this love
demand requires that I actively involve myself in service in
some way to my enemies and my friends rather than talking
about love from a safe distance? God's love is never at a distance; His love involves Him in our lives. As Karl Barth said,
"God is our Nearest."[4] Do I realize this?

If and when I find myself falling short of this love demand by
Jesus, I recognize where I am and where God wants me to be,
and recognize the difference between the two. I am judged. A
seminary professor prayed, "Lord, help us to see ourselves as we
really are; help us to see ourselves as you want us to be; and give
us the grace to make up the difference."

That difference breaks our hearts. We have sinned and fallen
"short of the glory of God" (Rom. 3:23). We are confronted by
our failure; and we repent, asking God to deal with us graciously. Thankfully, God does deal with us graciously and firmly. As
J. R. W. Stott wrote:

> Far from condoning sin, His love has found a way to expose it
> (because He is light) and to consume it (because He is fire) with-
> out destroying the sinner, but rather saving him.[5]

Stott's statement gives us a rather clear example of the relationship of love and judgment. They do not contradict one
another, rather, they are the same package. Judgment is a con-
suming fire that sears our spirits and causes us to cry out in
repentance. But judgment arises out of God's love as He calls
and demands that we be all that we are supposed to be, as He
calls us from where we are to where He wants us to be.

Expressed Love as Judgment

Not only does God judge by His truth, He also judges by definite expressions of love. As love is expressed in mercy and compassion, the most sinful and rebellious heart can be brought to repentance and change. Love's compassion and mercy show up darkness and meanness for what they really are, causing the sinner to either melt into repentance or flee. It can be a most uncomfortable and effective judgment. But, again, this is the kind of judgment which redeems if a person will accept it.

Simon Peter was unprepared for the events ahead. Jesus had warned him, and He also predicted Peter's denial. Peter did follow Jesus into the courtyard after Jesus' arrest. But during the course of the conversation around the fire, Peter denied Jesus three times. It was a dramatic and heartbreaking moment. The cock crowed, and—this is the poignant moment—Jesus "turned and looked at Peter." What was in that look? Something special, because Peter went out and "wept bitterly" from a broken heart (see Luke 22:54-63).

Disappointment was in that look. Jesus must have hoped for more from Peter, but Peter now had thrown away his commitments and convictions for the moment. Jesus felt deserted by a friend He hoped would be loyal. But behind the look was also love; that self-giving, accepting, forgiving love of Jesus for His impulsive disciple. One thing is certain, Simon Peter could not stay the same when he saw that look. All he could do for the moment was go out and weep bitterly. The compassion of Jesus had judged him.

How often has God's persistent love as expressed through a mother's love been the means by which a person was rescued from self-destructive acts or choices. One mother was very concerned about her son. However, since he was a college student and needed to accept responsibility for himself, she could not go get him and bring him home. She could no longer correct him as when he was a small child. In fact, to try to press her will upon him would have driven him farther away. As she talked about it, she made the statement, "I know that he is beyond my reach, but I know that he is not beyond God's reach." She did not say that with an easy sentimentality nor in judgment. She stated it as a firm conviction.

I believe that the mother was wrong in one sense about her son being beyond her reach. She had been a believer for years, and that love of God of which she spoke would have been expressed many times before the son was far from her. The love of God made known through her, I believe, did continue to be a guiding force in his life. The son, now successful in business, gives evidence of being a well-adjusted and happy individual.

A friend I met in seminary told me his story, especially about his rebelliousness during his college days. An outstanding football player, he used his prestige and intimidating size and strength to pretty much have his way. He threw caution and good judgment to the winds. He said, however, that during this time there was one disturbing image he could never quite escape, that of his mother praying. As he put it, "I had a praying mother." The image of his mother praying for him was an image of the deep love of God which finally led him back to his senses. Her love for her son became a demanding, exacting judgment of his antilove.

Warning as Judgment

A friend almost died as the result of an accident. As he lay on his hospital bed hanging between life and death, he displayed remarkable presence of mind and courage as he gave instructions about what was to be done about several family matters after he died. Miraculously, he recovered. Later, someone asked him how he knew he was about to die and thus knew to express his final requests about family matters. He said, "My body told me I was going to die. Your body tells you when you are going to die." Physicians seem to agree with this statement, and from what other patients have said, who were alert in a critical death-life condition, one's body does give that message of warning.

There seems to be a warning also from our spiritual side when we are doing wrong or about to do wrong. Some have called it conscience, but it is certainly more than a little voice which speaks inside of a person. Others call it culture conditioning, and to some degree that is often true, but is not adequate to explain the universal sense of right and wrong people naturally seem to have.

C. S. Lewis pointed out that this sense of right and wrong was designated by thinkers of old as a law of nature. This was before "laws of nature" came to refer to such laws as those dealing with gravitation, heredity, chemistry, or others. The older thinkers said the law was a law of *nature* because everyone knew the law without having to be taught it. It was innate—that is, the idea of decent behavior was known without decent behavior having to be defined. Of course, the older thinkers thought that there were exceptions to the general law, but, after all, they were expressing a general and not a specific law for the human race as a whole. Lewis, after much comparison and study, concluded that the general law is right. Whilethere are differences of moralities in different cultures, there is not a total difference.

He asked us to consider what a total difference would be like. Imagine a country in which you were praised for deserting your friends in a battle, or a situation in which double-crossing your friends would be an acceptable way of life. Even the person who denies that there is any absolute wrong or right is the first to demand to be treated fairly by others. How do you know what is fair?[6]

We, too, know basically what is fair. When we break, or are about to break, that "law of nature" we sense to some degree the wrong of our thoughts or actions. We are warned by our innate knowledge. I view this as a kind of judgment which God has made inherent in human nature. Of course, you have freedom to disobey this law just as you can disobey the law of gravitation or biological laws. To disobey however is to put yourself in great peril. If people attempt to deny or misuse the law of gravity, they can bring great harm or even death to themselves and to others. Even so, if we choose to do wrong, to disobey the innate law of decent behavior, we bring harm to ourselves and others.

In addition to this innate warning as a kind of judgment, the specific warnings abound. We are warned that "the wages of sin is death" (Rom. 6:23). Or, listen to this proverb of the Old Testament:

> The righteousness of the blameless
>   keeps his way straight,
> but the wicked falls by his own
>   wickedness.
> The righteousness of the upright
>   delivers them,
> but the treacherous are taken
>   captive by their lust.
> When the wicked dies, his hope
>   perishes,
> and the expectation of the
>   godless comes to nought (Prov. 11:5-7).

Or what about the Ten Commandments or a myriad of other warnings found in biblical and religious teaching? These are all warnings to us about the results of wrong choices and actions. God has, in reality, described the consequences beforehand in order to help us avoid negative actions and attitudes. The warning is preventative judgment. Again, God does not cause the negative consequences. They are the result of our own disobedience of that which is right. He judges wrong actions and attitudes for what they are and makes clear to us, for our benefit, the consequences inherent in such actions and attitudes.

Final Judgment: an Expression of Love?

While we give lip service to the idea that judgment is an expression of God's love, it is difficult for us to believe that at times. We cannot believe it if we lump together all bad things that happen to us as God's judgment. Also, it is difficult for us to accept judgment as love unless we understand the element of permitted judgment. Judgment that is permitted as the consequences of our own choices, individually and collectively, is judgment of our making.

But God even relates to permitted judgment in love. He works against the consequences of our sins, extending forgiveness and new beginnings. Also, God allows the negative consequences of our wrong choices not only because we are free, but because the consequences of unrighteousness should make us realize that we need to come to God's righteousness.

Even the final judgment where eternal separation takes place gives evidence of God's love. Again, it says to us that God loves enough to give us the freedom to choose, and ultimately to choose our own destiny. When that freedom can result in ultimate destruction, we should be inclined to take our freedom more seriously. Our choices ultimately are life-and-death matters.

Some, however, believe that God's love would not permit eternal death to be the destiny of a human being. They believe that ultimately everyone will be saved and will share eternal life with God. They believe that some will go through some severe punishment beyond death before they will come eventually to repentance and faith, but God will bring them to that point finally. No one ultimately will be lost, because to do so would be a defeat for God, and God cannot finally be defeated.

While I personally wish the view of universal salvation were true, I must warn that it is not. First, this view does not take seriously enough the real, terrible, wonderful freedom God has given human beings. God will ultimately take our freedom away, according to the Universalist's view, and He gives it to us now only to play around with for awhile. God ultimately can be defeated only at one point—He can be closed out of a person's life forever. If that reality did not exist, would freedom be real?

The view that punishment beyond this life eventually will bring a person to salvation speaks more of a works approach than a grace approach. Punishment, the Universalist may claim, will atone for a person's sins. However, the New Testament indicates that atonement for sins is an act of grace on God's part and that human beings are not capable of earning eternal life for themselves (see John 3:16; Eph. 2:8-9).

Also, against the Universalist's view, Jesus anticipated a final judgment and eternal separation from God. In Matthew 25:31-46, Jesus pictured Himself as the eternal Judge pronouncing a separation between those who are His and those who are not. The section ends with the statement of Jesus about those who are not His: "And they will go away into eternal punishment" (v. 46). I sometimes wish that our human freedom and responsibility were not so heavy, but they are. The sooner we realize it and dedicate ourselves to living in God's light, however, the more real living we will do. Again, real living is not a real possibility without that kind of freedom. The final judgment, then, in a negative sense, gives evidence of the love of God who gives us real freedom, even the freedom to build our own kingdom of destruction.

The acts of God's judgment are positive, as are the acts of judgment of a loving, earthly father, who disciplines his child, not to damage her, but to guide her correctly so she can have the best possible life. God's acts of judgment are perfect, for God's love is so much beyond what a human father or mother is capable of.

An Analogy of Judgment and Love

To demonstrate how judgment is an expression of love and how love becomes judgment, perhaps an analogy will help, although all analogies are limited when compared to the real thing. Consider a stream flowing in one direction. When a person dives into the stream, he has two choices. He can choose to swim with the flow of the stream, which always will flow in the same direction and never reverse itself. If he chooses to swim with the stream, the stream is his friend, it aids him; it lifts him and, with appropriate effort on his part, carries him to the destination he has chosen. But if he chooses to swim against the stream, the stream becomes his foe. It pushes against him, it exhausts him; his resistance to it causes him to bang against the rocks by the banks. It increasingly becomes a more miserable situation. In both cases the stream is the same. It is the choice of the person which determines whether it is friend or foe.

Allow the stream for a moment to represent in your thinking the flow of the life of God who is love. All of His created order flows in the same direction as that One of Love. He and His universe always will flow in the same direction. An individual in the flow of things—and no one can escape being in the flow— has two choices. You can go with the flow. God has marked out who you are, where you are going, and what your purposes are. And all of it is for the good of humankind. When you choose to go with God's flow, you recognize that you are in God's love. God's love sustains you, aids you, holds you up, and bears you toward a glorious destiny.

But suppose you go against the flow? Then you become like the person who tries to swim upstream. You exhaust yourself. You throw yourself against the love of God. The flow of God's love now becomes your enemy. It does not appear to be love to you, but judgment, even anger. Has God changed? Has God's love changed? No, but love has now become judgment to you who have thrown yourself against God. Only in this sense, it seems to me, is love an expression of judgment, and judgment an expression of love. Only in this sense is God against us. God is not of two natures; He is not schizophrenic. God is love; He is always love. It would be wonderful if you would turn around and go with the flow of God's love, but you can choose not to. Consequently, the love continues to be judgment to you.

To continue the analogy, not only do those attempting to go against the flow hurt themselves, they hurt others as well. They bump into others, obstruct the flow, and confuse others about the right direction. We are all in the flow together. To help one turn around, to go with the stream, is a high calling and responsibility which we have. But because we are all in the flow together, either going with it or contrary to it, the innocent also get hurt—get bumped and bruised. We run into anger and hatred, sometimes acting like that ourselves. We meet our enemies face to face. They—the confused, the haters, the hated, the enemies, the innocent, the foolish, the happy, the burdened—are all bound up in God's love together, for God loves all. God's way with us, including all persons, is the way of love.

We do not have to be afraid of God, then. He is not going to suddenly switch on us. With confidence that His judgment is always positive and never destroying or maiming, we can happily trust our lives to Him without hesitation. We can really know and believe that He is for us (Rom. 8:31), and we really can trust that in everything He works for our good (v. 28). We do need to fear our tendency to make harsh judgment for ourselves and others. We need to eagerly throw ourselves in a positive way into the stream of God's love. For God's way with us is the way of love.

Notes

1. John Baillie, *A Diary of Private Prayer* (London: Oxford University Press, 1972), p. 27

2. Thomas Harris, *I'm OK: You're OK* (New York: Harper & Row, 1967), pp. 35-53.

3. Lewis Smedes, *Love Within Limits* (Grand Rapids: William B. Eerdmans Publishing Company, 1978), p. 82.

4. Karl Barth, "Repentance," *The Protestant Pulpit,* ed. by A. W. Blackwood (New York: Abingdon Press, 1947), p. 173.

5. J. R. W. Stott, *The Epistles of John* (London: Hodder and Stoughton, 1966), pp. 160-161.

6. C. S. Lewis, *Mere Christianity* (New York: MacMillan Publishing Company, 1977) pp. 18-19.

9

Love and Death

"The best of all is, God is with us"; and then, as if to assert the faithfulness of our promise-keeping Jehovah and comfort the hearts of his weeping friends, lifting up his dying arm in token of victory and raising his feeble voice with a holy triumph not to be expressed, again repeated the heart-reviving words, "The best of all is, God is with us!" (From John Wesley's Last Hours).[1]

Where is God when we die? (Family of a patient).

God shows his love for us (Rom. 5:8).

Death is the noblest theme of poetry, narrative writing, and dramatic writing, or so said Elton Trueblood—and he seems to be accurate in his assessment. The two primary reasons he gave to support his claim also seem to be true. First, "Death is a greater leap in the dark than any other . . . we know and can know very little of what is on the other side of this chasm which we cross." Second, death is a universal experience. "This universality constitutes a marked difference between death and the other supremely revealing experiences of human life in that it is genuinely universal, while the others are nearly so."[2]

Marriage, parenthood, and fulfilling vocations are not the universal experience of all people. But every person knows he will die. Most disturbingly, every person knows his beloved will die. Rollo May wrote,

A man may have thought very little about death—and prided

himself on his "bravery"—until he becomes a father. Then he finds in his love for his child an experience of vulnerability to death: the Cruel Imposter can at any time take away the child.[3]

Reality

So, there it is; we have said it! We all die and so do those whom we love. We do not want to think about the reality or to face it; but since it is one of the common experiences of life which comes to us all, we really need to.

The reality is difficult to accept. D. P. Brooks noted that an earlier generation could be characterized as a death-defying group. Their songs looked beyond death to a deeper and better life: "There's a Land that Is Fairer Than Day," "When The Roll Is Called Up Yonder," "When We All Get to Heaven," and "When They Ring the Golden Bells." However, we moderns try to deny death as much as possible. We use euphemisms—"departed," "no longer with us," "passed away,"—for the word *death*, probably because it holds such mystery, sorrow, and sometimes horror for us that we do not want to say the word.[4]

In an episode of the television show "M*A*S*H," a pilot had been forced to eject from his crippled plane after a bombing run. He had only a slightly injured foot, and everything had been successful except for the loss of the plane. He limped into camp, and Hawkeye, the wacky but compassionate and capable physician, met him. The pilot explained to Hawkeye that he usually left his base, flew his mission, and then returned to his base to have dinner with his wife. Hawkeye asked if he had ever seen what happened when his bombs landed. The pilot had not. He explained how beautiful it was up there many thousands of feet above everything. The war was a very calm and somewhat unrealistic affair as far as the pilot was concerned. Only later at Hawkeye's instigation did he come face to face with what a bomb could do when he met a young girl who had been injured in a bombing raid. He was deeply shaken as he faced the reality of real war and the injury and death which bombs cause. We would like to stay above the reality of death, thinking somehow that we will not have to face it, but somewhere—somehow— something or someone will force us to the reality.

Death seems so undignified for us. We are supposed to stand on our own two feet and live. Consider this clinical description of death: "The absence of peripheral pulse and heartbeat, the absence of respiration, the lack of corneal reflex and the presence of a bluish color that results from a lack of oxygen in the blood."[5] How cold it seems to speak of a person in those terms; how undignified it sounds.

Death seems so useless. Four high school students in their car on the way to a high school play met a train at the railroad tracks and all were killed. They had so much promise—how uncalled for, and how unfair.

John and Donald Baillie, two Scottish theologians, are internationally known and respected. However, not very many know of their younger brother Peter. Peter was also a gifted and successful student who graduated with a degree in medicine. He went to India as a medical missionary. While still in language school, before he could really begin his medical career, he died in a drowning accident. His mother was crushed and so was her faith. Twice widowed, she had struggled valiantly and succeeded in putting her sons through Edinburg University. This senseless, useless death of Peter seemed to make her faith useless. Only through the care and ministry of her other two sons was she nursed back to faith.[6]

Death just doesn't seem to fit or belong. It is antilife. It is irrational. Especially does this become clear to us as we look at those whom we love. Trueblood pointed out Plato's struggle to come to grips with the death of Socrates.

> The ordinary good and thoughtful man does not begin, as some critics have supposed, by believing in immortality for himself because he, personally, desires it; he begins rather by noting the manifest injustice involved in the death of someone else and

drawing the necessary conclusion from the postulate that this is, in the end, a just world. Since justice is not done to some in this life, there must be another succeeding it; otherwise the very demand for justice is finally frustrated.[7]

In *Back to Methuselah,* George Bernard Shaw pictures Adam and Eve happening upon a fawn which has a broken neck and no longer lives. Eve decides to call it "dead," and Adam decides to throw the fawn into the river. They want to do away with the fawn because its dead condition is such an upsetting and unbearable sight. Shaw successfully communicates in this word picture how strange and shocking death is in the midst of life.[8]

Death can be a very undignified, useless, unnecessary, and alien event in this life. Nevertheless, it is a reality which we must face. Accepting the reality of death is necessary in order to deal with it in a healthy way.

Anxiety

There is an anxiety about death in many people, sometimes more on a subconscious than a conscious level. Rollo May believes that modern society's preoccupation with sex, as evidenced in today's humor, drama, economic interests, and advertising, is an attempt to repress the fear of death. The obsession with sex drains off the anxiety about death. He said,

> Death is the symbol of ultimate impotence and finiteness, and anxiety arising from this inescapable experience calls for the struggle to make ourselves infinite by way of sex. Sexual activity is the most ready way to silence the inner dread of death and, through the symbol of procreation, to triumph over it . . . What would we have to see if we could cut through our obsession about sex? That we must die. The clamor of sex all about us drowns out the ever-waiting presence of death.[9]

Some may be anxious because they feel that death is a tool used by God to punish, to have His way, or to get even for some reason. I have heard sermons that advocated that God will "wipe you out" if you get in His way. Granted, sinfulness may weigh a person's life down—so eat on his insides that because of stress or some other abuse from the wrong kind of living— that a death may be premature. But who among us does not many times stand over against the will of God and get in His way. We are all sinners, are we not?

Since some people have heard for so long that—upon the event of someone's death—"God took him" or "God called him home," or even, "He asked for it and God gave it to him," they are perplexed and even angry at God when the untimely and unexpected death of a loved one occurs. There is another avenue taken by this horrible theology: God punishes someone or takes out His wrath on someone by causing the death of someone else. After the death of his young wife in an automobile accident, the grief-stricken husband expressed the belief that because he was not the kind of person he was supposed to be, God took his wife.

It was out of such confusing ideas that the brilliant young Georgia Tech student cried, "Why?" in his grief over his father's death. His father had not seemed that ill, although he was in the hospital for treatment. Suddenly, however, he was dead. It was as if some power had reached in to wrench his father away from him and his mother. "Why?" he asked. "Why did God do this?"

I tried to explain some other possibility than God causing the death of his father. I fumbled for words and stumbled along in explanation. His father, I told him as gently as possible, had somewhat abused his body as all of us do in one way or another. His body and life had had a lot of wear and tear from stress and strain of different kinds, more so than his father or the doctors had realized. God had assisted his father's body in so many ways to give him longer life with them. But when the body could go no more, when the body had played out all its possibilities of sustaining life, he had died. At that point God "took" him and gathered him into eternal relationship with Himself and all the saints. No, God did not take his father from him and his mother. He did not want to cause them grief.

After several months of thinking, reading, and studying, the student was able to accept that God did not take his father from him. Also, he was able to feel once again that God really was *for* him. And that is important in anyone's life!

But why has death come to stalk life as it does if it is not God's tool He invented to use on human beings? Paul placed the fault on human sinfulness. He said that "sin came into the world through one man and death through sin, and so death spread to all men because all men sinned" (Rom. 5:12). The Old Testament expresses a similar conclusion in different places. The third chapter of Genesis, for example, gives the impression that after Adam's sin and expulsion from the Garden (Gen. 3:23) "his entire existence is placed under the sign of death. Thus man's labor and woman's childbearing carry with them an odor of death" (Gen. 3:16-20).[10]

Edmond Jacob suggested that the Hebrews believed that, since human beings were made of perishable matter (Gen. 3:-19), mortality belongs to the natural experience of humanity. He concluded, however, that the garden and the fall of Adam and Eve into sin may suggest that

> had man persevered in obedience to God by respecting the divine commands, God would have reserved the right to change man's condition and grant him immortality as a favor. Man's disobedience irremediably destroyed this possibility, and thenceforth death, which until that time had been virtual, became an actuality for him.[11]

While the Bible does not say, "This and this is the ultimate origin of death" (Paul said that death only came into human existence through sin), it is evident that sin is an enemy of humankind and thus an enemy of God. Death is evil (Deut. 30:15,19); it is horrific (Ps. 55:4f), and it is bitter (1 Sam. 15:32), which led Alan Richardson, in his *A Theological Wordbook of the Bible,* to say that death is unnatural. Whatever the case, it is plain that the Bible views death as being against the good of humankind.[12]

Deliverance

So, we need deliverance. But deliverance is something we have to accept, it is not something we make. People try to make a deliverance of some kind. Beyond simply denying one's mortality, other methods of deliverance from the reality and effects of death have been and are being attempted. Various forms of embalming in the past have been attempts to preserve personhood in some kind of way. The modern practice of immediately freezing the body at death is an attempt to preserve life. Those frozen are there to be repaired and brought back to life in the future, assuming that science will advance to the point where that kind of thing can be done. Such people must have viewed life as being only biological in nature, which is a rather simplistic and inadequate view of personhood.

Still others look upon death itself as the final event and consequently a deliverance—but a deliverance to what? Being delivered from something to nothingness is not really a deliverance, it is nothing. Even being "remembered" as one who made a contribution in this life does not carry with it any sense of deliverance. The problem of death still has not been answered, and it is a problem which demands a reasonable answer. I remember the consternation I felt when I heard a man say that he believed in an eternal God but not eternity for human beings. God is eternal, but life is all over for human beings at death, he claimed. The only thing that lives after a person is the good or evil he has done for his fellow human beings. It seemed to me that he had reached a new high in inconsistency when he spoke of an eternal God but no possibility of eternal life for a human being.

The Christian faith views life as more than mere biological existence. To perceive a human life as merely a collection of cells functioning in relationship to other-collections of cells around it is preposterous. That a person is created in the image of God (Gen. 1:27) means for the Christian faith that a life, a person, has eternal potential. We are beings in relationship to the eternal, and that relationship is characterized by love, *agapē* love, especially from God's side. As the apostle Paul said, nothing separates "us from the love of God in Christ Jesus our Lord" (Rom. 8:39).

It is in chapter 8 of Romans that God's love and the problem of death are brought into close relationship. Anders Nygren has pointed out a development in Paul's argument in chapters 5 through 8 of Romans which is important for our consideration about God's love and death.[13] Paul, according to Nygren, emphasized what a person who is in Christ is freed from: chapter 5—freedom from wrath; chapter 6—freedom from sin; chapter 7—freedom from the law; and chapter 8—freedom from death. Chapter 8, of course, is pivotal. You can have the other freedoms, but unless you are freed from death you are not really freed at all. Freedom from death is a necessity if a human being is to really live.

So what is the key to this freedom from death? The key is not to be found from our side but from God's side. The answer to the question is this: God is *for* us! (Rom. 8:31). All of chapter 8 is about that truth. Nygren said, and this is important, "And that God is for us does not merely mean that He is graciously disposed toward us. Above all it means that He is for us in what He *does*."[14]

God does not simply sit on His throne, view us, and say, "Those stumbling, bumbling people I really like—I feel good about them. I am relaxed about them. Somehow they will make it." No, remember the description of *agapē* love, the kind of love with which God loves us. It is self-giving; it is donated life. It is life giving itself in behalf of another. We speak of incarnation, God coming in Christ to live among us. Why did He come in Christ? Because He wanted to get involved with us, to do with us and do for us. God overcame the distance and the separateness that we cause in our relationship with Him.

We must overcome our separateness. Eric Fromm claimed that since a person is gifted with reason, he is life becoming aware of itself. He realizes that he came into the world without his decision, and he will leave this world without his will. Those he loves will die before him or he before they. There are forces beyond his control in both nature and society. He is aware of his aloneness and separateness, and this separateness makes a prison for him. Unless one can unite with the world outside, the failure to overcome this separateness results in insanity. The insane person withdraws from the world so radically that that from which he is separated, the world outside, disappears as far as he is concerned. The denial of the reality of the world outside is a condition of insanity. How does one overcome this separateness? Fromm indicated that by reunion with humanity through love one overcomes the separateness.[15]

The biblical claim that we are separated from God is the ultimate separation which must be overcome. Human beings sense that this life is limiting and incomplete. They sense the eternal nature of things. So they do desire to overcome the separateness that exists between them and God. Or if they have no idea of God, they desire to penetrate the mystery of the ultimate unknown, such as death and its aftermath. God has taken the initiative to overcome the separateness. He has eliminated all distance by coming to us in His Son, Jesus Christ. That is an act of love. Union or reunion, as the case may be, really can occur only by God's act of love toward us and our response of acceptance. Eternal love overcomes the eternal separateness. God is intimately involved with us because His whole being is an action of love acting upon and intimately involved with our lives.

But, alas, does not death break that reunion, causing the separateness to exist once again? No, God's love is a living relationship between God and us. God overcomes the power of death by the power of His love, His outgoing life intimately tied up with ours and acting on our part. The resurrection of Christ demonstrated this reality. All the evil of this world could not overcome God's love and life as made known in Christ Jesus.

Paul affirmed the reality. He gathered up in his mind all the powers which he could think of, all the things that could separate from God—tribulation, distress, persecution, famine, nakedness, peril, sword, death, life, angels, principalities, things present, things to come, height, depth, or anything else—and said that nothing is "able to separate us from the love of God in Jesus Christ our Lord" (see Rom. 8:35-39). The living relationship of love is never broken, not even by something so seemingly final as death.

Becoming

Death, as far as the Christian is concerned, can be looked upon as part of one's becoming. It is process. It is a stage of growth. My lovely wife and I were talking about death, and she put it this way: "Dying is a part of living." We die in order to become something else, in order to move along in the pilgrimage.

We die every day. Carlyle Marney said that his little girls taught him this. As they left on a vacation, they would say "good-bye" to such things as the trees and the house as they experienced a kind of death—a separation from part of themselves.[16] We leave behind friends as we move away. We leave behind teachers as we move from grade to grade in school. We watch brothers and sisters go away from home as they take on the world for themselves. All of these experiences mean that we die some, a little at the time.

But such events are necessary. We need to move to new teachers. New responsibilities take us to new places and we must accept that deathlike separation from friends. Brothers and sisters must go away in order to fulfill their lives. All of these experiences are experiences of dying into additional growth.

However, we do not hasten the dying. We realize that we must live before we die. We are to live out every ounce of our strength and life before we can die into more growth. That is our responsibility. Suicide, in whatever form it takes, is not the way to go. The onslaught of disease and accidents that cause death are interruptions of the living and dying process.

However, God takes those and turns them into growth as well. We cannot do anything about the accidents once they have happened, but God does something about the results of accidents to His children—He calls His children to continued growth in His presence.

John 1:12 says, "But to all who received him . . . he gave power to become children of God." Marney had an interesting translation of this statement by which he preserved the Greek verb action: *"To everyone who took him in* (once for all as if to keep forever) *in them did he release* (once for all) *the power to go on becoming Godlike."*[17]

We can go on becoming "godlike" no matter what. Hans Schwarz was so bold as to write: "It is a sign of the goodness of creation that we are able to die and to cease from being dimensionally separated from our creator."[18] He went on to say that death is the termination of distortions, of our tie to sinfulness and antigodly character. It is a final "no" to our alienation from God.[19] Niebuhr quoted Luther about two great future blessings in death:

> "The first, in that through death the whole tragedy of this world's ills is brought to a close. . . . The other blessing of death is this, that it not only concludes the pains and evils of this life, but (which is more excellent) makes an end of sins and vices. . . . For this our life is so full of perils—sin, like a serpent, besetting us on every side—and it is impossible for us to live without sinning, but fairest death delivers us from these perils, and cuts our sin clean away from us."[20]

This is not to say that death is good. It is to say that God's love, which is God intimately involved for the good of others in the experiences of life, neutralizes death. It has no "sting" in it. The grave has no "victory" at all over God's children. Death is both change and continuation, as D. P. Brooks said. He wrote, "From the earthly side, death is destruction, dissolution. But from the other side, death is passage, a bridge to eternity for those who belong to Christ."[21]

Death is part of the process of growth by which we come fully into relationship with God. God, then, out of His love for us— God who is for us with all of His being and doing—overcame death, something which we were and are powerless to ultimately do anything about, and turned it into a step of growth. He does this by loving us, by tying His life so intimately with ours that, if we are willing, by His power He can raise us up to the eternal. We are raised up, we grow, beyond the limits of our once-limited life. We are given a new house: "For we know that if the earthly tent we live in is destroyed, we have a building from God, a house not made with hands, eternal in the heavens" (2 Cor. 5:1).

I delight in Paul's continuing development of his thought after this passage. He was saying that he longed for the fulfillment of living in this house made by God, "so that what is mortal may be swallowed up by life" (v. 4). We grow from mortal into God's kind of life—"swallowed up by God's life." We are headed, then, as God's children, toward the ultimate growth which has unlimited potential because the present boundaries of our limited house will die and we will be granted a life we cannot even begin to imagine. How great is God's *agapē!*

Notes

1. Betsy Ritchie, "Wesley's Last Hours," in *The Journal of John Wesley,* ed. by Percy L. Parker (Chicago: Moody Press, n.d.), p. 419.

2. Elton Trueblood, *The Common Ventures of Life* (New York: Harper & Row, 1949), p. 105.

3. Rollo May, *Love and Will* (New York: W. W. Norton & Co., 1969) p. 102.

4. D. P. Brooks, *Dealing with Death—A Christian Perspective* (Nashville: Broadman Press, 1974), p. 13.

5. Hans Swartz, *On the Way to the Future* (Minneapolis: Augsburg Publishing House, 1972), p. 164.

6. Leonard Griffith, *Gospel Characters* (Grand Rapids: William B. Eerdmans Publishing Co., 1976), p. 76.

7. Trueblood, *The Common Ventures*, p. 106.

8. See Carlyle Marney, *Faith in Conflict* (New York: Abingdon, 1957), p. 122.

9. Rollo May, *Love and Will*, p. 106. D. P. Brooks in *Dealing With Death* reminded me of this emphasis.

10. Edmond Jacob, "Death," in *The Interpreter's Dictionary of the Bible*, I, ed. by G. A. Buttrick (New York: Abingdon Press, 1962), p. 803.

11. Ibid.

12. Alan Richardson, "Death," in *A Theological Word Book of the Bible*, ed. by Alan Richardson (New York: The Macmillan Co., 1967), p. 60.

13. Lee Anders Nygren, *Commentary on Romans*, trans. by Carl C. Rasmussen (Philadelphia: Fortress Press, 1949), pp. 191-346.

14. Ibid, p. 347.

15. Eric Fromm, *The Art of Loving* (New York: Bantam Books, 1972), pp. 6-8.

16. Maurney, *Faith in Conflict*, p. 141.

17. Ibid, p. 139.

18. Swartz, *Future*, p. 167.

19. Ibid.

20. H. Richard Niebuhr, *Christ and Culture* (New York: Harper & Row, 1951), pp. 178-179.

21. Brooks, *Dealing with Death*, p. 93.

10

God's Love
Means God Is for You

The declaration is that God and man correspond each to the other: man is a spirit, and so is God: "spirit with Spirit can meet," and only in such meeting is there genuine worship. So whenever the human spirit seeks the divine, the divine may be found, whether in a so-called sacred place or not; for the divine is indeed a Spirit, that knows and loves and acts without such limits of time and space as confine the human. (William Newton Clarke).[1]

Is God really for me? (The counselee).

God shows his love for us (Rom. 5:8).

She stood apart from the crowd—isolated, alone, and fearful. A look of desperation was on her face. It was the kind of desperation, however, which galvanizes the will into determination. When the crowd had its attention riveted on Jesus, when the clamor and the movement were such that no one noticed her, she moved swiftly into the crowd. At a point when she was close enough to Jesus, she reached past the bodies and legs of others, stretching to the fullest length of her arm, and touched the hem of His garment. The woman immediately received the full attention of Jesus (Matt. 9:20-22).

Of course, she did not realize at first that she was one for whom Christ came. God, coming into the world in Christ, was for her. We can identify with her inability to understand that

God in Christ was for her, because many of us have had difficulty in accepting the truth that God is for us.

Some believe that God is not for them because they simply have been too bad. Others feel that they are really insignificant. Some will affirm that God is for them, but it is only mental affirmation that they make, little realizing the impact of what they say they believe. Others may affirm that God is for them, but do so because that is what they are supposed to believe although they may be very unsure about the actual reality. Finally, there are those who do not believe that God exists, so they, sadly, cannot know that God is for them too.

To know that God is for you, to not only mentally affirm the fact but feel and accept that God is for you is a great experience. You have been doing battle with whatever forces in your life, and you are losing. Suddenly the cavalry has arrived with reinforcements so vast and strong the enemy flees in terror. Oh, the battle is not over yet, but it is an altogether different battle now because you know that God is for you.

You have been walking in darkness, stumbling along because you cannot see. The darkness is so heavy and vast that you have no hope of ever getting out of it. Then, suddenly, the light is everywhere, and the darkness is fleeing as the night runs from the rising sun. Now you can see, because you know—you feel it—that God is for you.

We Can Believe that God Is for Us

Consider the evidence. God is Creator. What did He create? We at least know that He created the world. But for whom? For Himself? Did God need a world? Of course not. God created a world so that He could fit us with it. He clothed us with all kinds of support systems and resources so that we could be sustained.

The created order is for us. We did not bring it with us when we arrived. Neither did we make it. In fact, we did not even make ourselves. We are a part of, and at the same time, the crowning act of His creation. We even have been given dominion over creation (Ps. 8:5-8). When we do not misuse creation, trying to shape it into something for selfish ends, and when we do not bow down and worship creation, it fits us. Creation is for us because God is for us.

We can be grateful, for example, for gravity and the way it fits us. I am glad that when I stumble and fall, I know in which direction I am going to fall. Think how complicated life would be if it were not for the fact that we always fall downward. What if we fell sideways or upward? I suppose that we would have to remove some things from the ceilings and walls in our homes that would be extremely dangerous if we fell against them. It is somewhat reassuring to know that when we arrive home to our families we do not wonder whether they will be plastered against the ceiling or sitting on the walls. We can be reasonably sure that we will encounter them at floor level somewhere.

Think how complicated it would be to place a table lamp if it were not for gravity. I know that I am not to attempt to set a lamp on the side of the table, or underneath the table. I set the lamp on the table. It is as simple as that. Of course, our astronauts are learning how to exist in a gravity-free environment—and God has given us the wonderful ability to adapt to and use our environment in a good way—but it is a complex and difficult existence. The creation is for us. God is for us.

The incarnation—God coming in Jesus Christ to dwell among us—is for us. Did He need to come and dwell among us in order to do something for Himself? Did He walk among us, sharing our common pains, sorrows, and sufferings, as well as our joys, in order to please Himself? It is obvious that He did not do this for Himself—He came for us.

Paul wrote this wonderful statement in Philippians 2:7 about Christ coming to share life with us. He said that Christ "emptied" Himself. The Greek word for *emptied* means to pour out all the contents of a vessel. While this statement has many theological implications, it certainly means that Christ did not grasp for a higher position but gave us what He had. It was necessary for Him to give up His divine preogatives to really enter into our human situation.

He took on, as Paul wrote, the "form of a servant," or actually the form of a "slave." He came to serve humanity, not to be ministered unto but to minister (Mark 10:45). Again, God was in Christ reconciling the world to Himself (2 Cor. 5:19). This means that God was acting in Christ. Therefore, God Himself in His Son assumed the role of a servant to humankind.

We perhaps have heard reference to Christ's role as servant so many times that we have lost the significance of its impact. God is Sovereign, Ruler, and Maker of all the universe. We could understand God coming with a display of might and majesty, even appearing with a host of warriors to stamp out all evil. Or, perhaps in a more modern picture, using His power to manipulate the atoms of matter so that any flaw in His creation was simply dissipated or corrected without concern for individuals. But no, the eternal God came in His Son to serve you and me. And He serves us only in ways that are good for us. All of this should not surprise us, because God is love, a love which expends life in behalf of others.

In *The Agony and the Ecstasy,* Irving Stone told of Michelangelo's creation of the mighty statue of David. He began with a column of marble seventeen feet high and weighing two thousand pounds. Other sculptors had given up on the marble block, because it had been gouged so deeply midway of its height that they said it would break in two. However, Michelangelo designed his statue of David so that the hips could be swiveled into the good part of the stone and the flawed part could be eliminated. Then the master sculptor went to work, finding such joy in his task that he hardly stopped to eat or rest. He chipped away, knocking off the rough edges, shaping, and rounding, until the figure of the magnificent *David* began to push itself out of the mass of marble. The master sculptor turned a flawed piece of marble into a magnificent statue of David.[2]

God came among us in His Son, and He began to chip away

the rough edges of people, and to smooth out the rough places. He eliminated the flawed places by His forgiveness. Under His touch, all people have the possibility of expressing themselves out of their experiences as the unique and gifted persons they are. God is *for* us. The incarnation tells us that.

The crucifixion is for us. God was in Jesus even on the cross. Why? Did God need to do battle with sin and death in order to defeat them for Himself? Those sins for which Christ died (1 Cor. 15:3), were they His sins? God did none of that for Himself; it was all for us. The crucifixion says clearly that God is for us.

Some people may reason that since Christ took upon Himself their sins that they caused His death. However, our sins did not *make* Him go to the cross. He had power to take up or lay down his life (John 10:18). He went to the cross not to condemn us but to deliver us. To continue to carry guilt for one's sins is a denial of what Christ accomplished on the cross. It is the refusal of the gift of forgiveness which Christ willingly and joyfully offers to us. He accepted and endured the cross because He was *for* us with his whole being—His willing, His thinking, His feeling were for us.

The resurrection is for us. God in Christ demonstrated His victory and superiority over death, the most potent enemy of humankind. God raised up Jesus, and in doing so liberated His Son from the limiting boundaries of this imperfect life. And Jesus came to tell us that we are all children of God. We are brothers and sisters with Christ. God wants His sons and daughters with Him, freed from the limiting boundaries of this life. In that way we are always moving from grace to grace (see John 1:16) and not even death can stop that pilgrimage. By the resurrection, God brings us into the fullness of His grace. The resurrection proclaims that God is for us.

As we look at the great events of God's action in human history, there is not one which was not done for His children. Creation, calling of Israel into existence as His people, Old Testament revelation, incarnation, life of Jesus, crucifixion, resurrection, calling of the church into existence, New Testament revelation, and the continuing evidences of His action in our lives all give irrefutable evidence that God is for us. Can we accept that with gratitude in our own thinking, willing, and feeling?

God Is For Us During the Bad Times

At times the glory of God is overwhelming, evident. Things seem right and in balance, and it is easy to sing of the blessings of God.

The pilot said that we were twenty-three thousand feet up. We were above the clouds which looked like layers and mountains of pure snow, or as one passenger remarked rather loudly, "big bales of white cotton." It was early and the sunlight was glancing off the clouds, bathing some of them with a red tinge. The sun made everything brighter. The sun also tinged the sky, highlighting various shades of blue, white, and pink. It was altogether a beautiful sight. It was rather easy to look at that scene and to think that this is really a good and beautiful world which fits us. Since I was thinking of this chapter in this book on that flight, it was easy for me to take the next step and think that such beauty shouts out to me that God is for me.

However, things did not remain that way. Soon we were making our descent through the clouds. The clouds were all around us. The plane shook as it passed through some turbulence. We could not see, and we knew that the pilot could not see.

Although things were rather routine, there was a slight but perceptible mood change among the passengers. Because of the clouds all around us and because we could not see as well as we could above the clouds, were most of us contemplating the precariousness of our existence? It seemed to be true. The same passenger who had remarked about the clouds looking like great bales of cotton now said, from several rows back, "It's all in the hands of the Man."

When we were above the clouds, I could think of praising God. However, when we were in the clouds, I thought more of asking for God's help and protection. I thought of human weakness and limitation. How silly of human beings to think they can keep an airplane that big up that high for that long! I needed God in a somewhat different way in the clouds than I did when we were above the clouds.

That airline flight is a parable about life. It is much easier to feel that God is for us and in control when the sun is shining and things are in balance with seemingly no threats on the horizon. But when things seem threatening, ominous, we may not be so certain that God is for us.

The chapters of this book deal with some of those times. The obvious presence of evil, the experiences of suffering, the experiences of negative judgment, the absence of community, the sense of personal failure, all may be times when people do not feel that God is for them.

However, even when the clouds are around, God is for us. As we plummeted through the blanket of clouds toward our landing spot, I realized that although the pilot could not see, he was flying the airplane. He did so because the flight of the airplane was tied into the realities of the created order, realities that relate to gravity, velocity, space, distance, and so forth. Even when the clouds are all around, there are evidences that God is for us.

Fosdick emphasized that we find God in unlikely places.[3] Moses' life as an adult had been something of a stream of unfortunate experiences. He ended up in the wilderness, tending the flocks of Jethro, his father-in-law. Not only was he in the wilderness physically, his life was in the wilderness. In that unlikely place, which must have seemed to him to be the wasteland of life, he had the burning bush experience. The wilderness was penetrated by God who was for him (Ex. 3:2-4).

The wilderness was an unlikely place for God to meet Moses, especially in the unlikely occurrence of a bush which burned but was not consumed. Moses decided that he would turn "aside and see." God's people everywhere can be glad that Moses did turn aside to see, because he became the means of so much of God's work and revelation from which we all have been blessed. Think of his leadership of the people of Israel out of bondage. Because of that event, we understand a great deal about how God redeems and delivers us. Think of the Ten Commandments which came through Moses. The whole world has benefitted from those Commandments. Dr. J. Hardee Kennedy, in his book *The Commission of Moses and the Christian Calling,* said of Moses that "it may be said in truth that he lived so well . . . the world has not been able to forget that he lived."[4] I am glad that Moses turned aside to see.

But what about us? Moses perhaps was seeking God, trying at least to understand something of the meaning and purpose of life and his life in particular. He discovered, however, out of the burning bush experience, that God was seeking him. God also seeks us. Perhaps there are a number of "burning bushes" we have walked by out of which God could reveal Himself. Because of our insensitivity to God's work in and around our lives we miss the evidence that He knows us and cares about us. He is not hiding from us nor is He against us.

God is for us. Even in the storm clouds when we cannot see where we are going, we can tie into the Ultimate Reality who keeps us on course. God penetrates our darkness, our wilderness. Even in those times we can be assured that God is for us.

We Can Be for Ourselves

Return to the woman who touched the hem of Jesus' garment. Her life was in a pitiful state. Because she had the hemorrhage, she was considered unclean by others. To touch her was to become ritually unclean. She must have felt the rejection deeply. How could she avoid feeling badly about herself? And if her religion relegated her to the status of outcast, she must have believed she was unfit for God and therefore rejected by God. On a scale of zero to ten, her sense of acceptance was zero.

However, when she touched the hem of Jesus' garment, Jesus stopped, and, in so doing, stopped everything. Imagine that the crowd stopped, became quiet, and everything was frozen in place. The woman who intended not to be noticed became the center of attention. For a moment suspended in time, a moment which took on eternal proportions, she not only was the center of the crowd, but the center of the whole universe, because Jesus turned and looked at her. These were the eyes of God, the One around whom the whole universe revolves, looking at her and understanding her.

Did He say to her, "Get away from Me you unclean woman," or "Don't you see that I am busy? Don't bother Me." No, nothing in His manner communicated to her that she was unworthy or unimportant. Rather, the opposite was true. He said to her, "Daughter"—which implies to me: "You are My family. You are significant. You are as important as anyone in this world, and that is very important. You are My very own."

That woman must have thought very highly of herself after that. Not in a self-centered way, of course, because the way God gives us reason to think highly of ourselves also enables us to think highly of others. But she must have gone away being for herself.

It is difficult for us to think of being for ourselves, or to put it more clearly, to love ourselves. We are conditioned to think otherwise. While it is considered proper to love others, we have been taught that it is very improper to love ourselves.

One of the major influences in Western thought is the stream of thought from John Calvin, the sixteenth-century Reformer. There is much good in this stream of thought but some bad. For example, Calvin, according to Erich Fromm, identified self-love and selfishness as being the same. So did Sigmund Freud, according to Fromm. Freud represents another stream of thought which has had a major impact on Western thought. Love and self-love are mutually exclusive according to Freud's understanding. The more there is of self-love, the less there is of love.[5]

Fromm taught that selfishness exists because there is an absence of self-love. No true concept of a human being applies to others if it does not apply to each one of us. Fromm emphasized that rather than being the same thing, self-love and selfishness are opposites.[6]

Certain applications can be drawn from Fromm's emphasis. If I believe that a human being is a person of dignity and value, then I also should believe that I am a person of dignity and value, for I am a human being. If I believe that every person is deserving of love, then I should believe that I also am deserving of love, for I am a person. In fact, believing that I am a person of dignity and value who is deserving of love—and thus loving myself—is necessary before I can believe that others are of dignity and value, and love them.

If I believe that I am not worthy of acceptance, then I will not accept others. If I consider myself to be lowly and worthy of rejection and unhappiness, I will inevitably treat others in the same way. If I practice hating myself, putting myself down, then I will treat others the same way. If I disparage my talents and contributions, if I find nothing about me to be unique and important, I will inevitably treat others in the same way—perhaps not all others in each case, but certainly many others. In short, if I do not love myself, I cannot love others. Self-love is OK. It is all right to be for ourselves. That is the best way to be for others.

Of course, Jesus taught that we should "love your neighbor as yourself" (Luke 11:27) long before Fromm. Many of us, however, have missed the "as yourself" part of that Commandment. We really cannot love our neighbor until we love ourselves. It is OK to be for ourselves.

I admire the woman who touched the hem of Jesus' garment. She did not have much self-esteem since she was a social outcast. She really did not have much faith. She probably did not understand much about Jesus and His identity and purpose. Her faith may have been small. She did believe that He was an important person who somehow might be able to meet her need.

Although she must have reasoned that she was not important and worthy, there was something inherent in her nature which caused her to say, "I am at least significant enough to reach out and touch the hem of his garment without Him or anyone else knowing. I am at least that important."

She did not beat down with all sorts of excuses and disparaging remarks that one small thought of self-esteem. That she was at least worthy enough to touch the hem is the kind of thought the Spirit of God would put in a person, propelling that person in the direction of Jesus. She allowed that thought to rise to the surface, and she acted upon it.

I imagine that God wishes that we would do at least as much as the woman. As He loves us, which is His way with us, He also urges us to love ourselves. He also urges us toward His Son in whom he Expresses His love for us, as when Jesus looked at the woman and said to her, "Daughter."

God is for us. We can be for ourselves. We can be for others. God loves us. We can love ourselves. We can love others. It is all tied up together. But it all begins and has begun with God who is love, and whose very way with us is the way of love.

Notes

1. William Newton Clarke, "God as Personal," in *Christian Classics: Nineteenth Century Evangelical Theology,* ed. by Fisher Humphreys (Nashville: Broadman Press, 1981), p. 115.

2. Irving Stone, *The Agony and the Ecstasy, Best Sellers from Reader's Digest Condensed Books* (Pleasantville, N. Y., The Reader's Digest Association, 1961), pp. 226-233.

3. Harry Emerson Fosdick, *What Is Vital in Religion* (New York: Harper & Brothers, 1955), pp. 1 *ff.*

4. J. Hardee Kennedy, *The Commission of Moses and the Christian Calling* (Grand Rapids: Wm. B. Eerdmans Publishing Company, 1964), p. 12.

5. Fromm, *The Art of Loving* (New York: Bantam Books, 1972), pp. 48-49.

6. Ibid., pp. 50-53. 50-53.